P9-CFT-100
7
11で

Inside Corporate Japan

"This book has been written by a highly regarded authority and is indispensable for anyone doing business in Japan. Dr. Lu has cut through a lot of the nonsense we hear about Japanese business and its methods, and tells us what really gives successful Japanese companies their edge...and how these same methods can be adopted by competing American and European companies."

—George Fields, author of *From Bonsai to Levis*

Inside Corporate Japan
The Art of Fumble-Free Management

David J. Lu

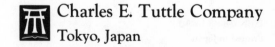 Charles E. Tuttle Company
Tokyo, Japan

The author is grateful for permission to use excerpts from the following:
Made in Japan: Akio Morita and Sony by Akio Morita with Edwin
M. Reingold and Mitsuko Shimomura. Copyright © 1986 by E. P. Dutton.
Reprinted by permission of the publisher, E. P. Dutton, a division of
NAL Penguin, Inc.

Published by the Charles E. Tuttle Company, Inc.
of Rutland, Vermont & Tokyo, Japan
with editorial offices at
2-6 Suido 1-chome, Bunkyo-ku, Tokyo 112
by special arrangement with Productivity Press

© 1987 by David J. Lu

All rights reserved

First Tuttle edition, 1989
Third printing, 1991

ISBN 0-8048-1609-3
Printed in Japan

Contents

Acknowledgments

I wish to thank the many Japanese friends who kindly responded to my questions during extensive interviews. My first impulse is to list everyone, but a number have agreed to interviews only if their names and affiliations are not made public. To be just, I have reluctantly decided not to publish any names. However, I want these friends to know how much I appreciate their kind assistance.

One person, however, requires public recognition. Ms. Watanabe Yuriko, formerly of the Naigai News Company and now a director of Zennponsha Publishing, made numerous arrangements for me to visit Japanese companies and interview their executives. While I was away from Japan, she also served as a "clearinghouse" for communication from my Japanese friends. Without her assistance, I would have missed many opportunities and a good deal of information.

I also wish to thank Norman Bodek and his capable staff at Productivity Press, Inc. From the time the manuscript was submitted to him to its publication, only four months have elapsed. He and his staff have worked on this book diligently and provided valuable professional assistance. The manner in which this book is produced reminds me of the best in Japanese management techniques, with visual control and other means effectively utilized. Indeed, whatever Japan can do, so can we, and this book is dedicated to this common cause with thanks to all.

David J. Lu

Preface

This is a book about Japan and about Japanese companies. I like to think of it as a book that opens a *shoji* screen to give an insider's view of Japanese boardrooms, offices and workplaces, along with some hints about behavior patterns. *Shoji* is a latticed sliding screen covered with translucent paper. When a room is enclosed by a *shoji*, the outside is not visible but light still enters through the screen, giving a soft glow. On a sunny day, trees and passers-by can cast shadows over the screen and even into the room. People inside the room are conscious of what is happening outside without actually seeing it. When the *shoji* is opened, however, the entire panorama of the outside world suddenly becomes part of the room. In some ways, Japanese companies are very much like a room with a *shoji*. While one aspect is hidden from the outside, though not always consciously, another can be wide open. And at times the two may converge.

Please do not think that Japanese companies are mysterious and different. The veil of mystery is like a morning mist that will clear when the sun rises. In fact, as much as 80 percent of their operations may be the same as those in U.S. companies. They have computer terminals and secretarial pools. They have board and stockholder meetings. They have purchasing divisions that maintain close contact with suppliers and inspect their quality. We are in many ways alike. But the issue here is how different the remaining 20 percent can be, and what impact this 20 percent may have on American companies. To investigate this 20 percent is to know what makes Japanese companies tick. Here are some points to look for:

1. Japanese companies learn how to be competitive at home, nurtured well by regional markets like Tokyo, Nagoya and Osaka. But at the same time, they also learn to support one another when meeting a foreign competitor. (Chapter 1)

2. Emphasis on human resources is intense. Japanese recruitment and training methods ensure that their emloyees become good team players. The layers of responsibilities are minimal and they can move more decisively. (Chapter 2)

3. Japan's record of labor peace is reinforced through frequent appeal to the company's corporate philosophy and culture. Even in major corporations, there is an effort to maintain a family-like atmosphere. Management is less politicized, and management by example is practiced. (Chapter 3)

4. Many Japanese companies have perfected the art of cost cutting with precision. When push comes to shove, *voila!*, another quality product at an even lower cost. (Chapter 4)

5. There is a genuine commitment to total quality control (TQC) from the president down to line workers. Its practice breaks down walls of separation found in many companies. With TQC, dissemination of essential information becomes much easier. (Chapter 5)

6. A company is not just a profit-making organization. It must discharge its social obligations. Successful companies are community-, employee- and customer-oriented. (Chapter 6)

Many Japanese practices are worth emulating, while others provide food for thought. At the end of each chapter, I have included a section called "Reflections." It derives its inspiration from conversations with those Japanese friends, from prime ministers and CEOs to line workers, who kindly shared their views with me for this book. They view the decline of American industry with alarm and offer some concrete suggestions. They are courteous and muffle their criticism with kind words, but the implication is clear. "Why can't you do it more efficiently?" "We learned these methods from Americans, but now the students are doing better than their teachers," and so on.

In writing these "Reflections," I have chosen not to give a long treatise. Instead, they are in the form of checklists. I hope that, as you read them, you will think about your surroundings and what can be done to improve them.

When you go to Japan, you may want to know how far you must bow (15, 30 or 45 degrees), where to sit and so on. The appendix on Japanese etiquette is inspired by a superb handbook written by IBM Japan. Observance of these simple rules can make your stay in Japan a more pleasant one and help you conclude your trade talks successfully.

You may ask why it is necessary to study Japanese practices. A simple answer is that you cannot afford not to know! You may have a prosperous business, but decisions made in Tokyo can change your fortune overnight. Had the television manufacturers, steelmakers and automakers known more about Japan, the state of our economy today might be quite different.

Having known both countries well, I never cease to be amazed by the difference in response the two countries give to a similar set of circumstances. A spectacularly successful year by American standards may be treated in Tokyo as a normal year with further improvement required, while a run-of-the-mill year by Japanese standards may be treated by an American company as another banner year. The former fosters an attitude of "improvement after improvement" and the latter one of complacency.

Perhaps we have been too complacent as individuals as well as institutions. Chapter 8, the concluding chapter, deals with trade policy issues. It offers some suggestions on how the government might help industries regain their competitiveness. It deals with currency realignment and a host of other options and suggests that limited protection may be offered to certain key sectors. The criterion for selecting the right or wrong approach, however, is whether or not a given measure is able to promote individual initiatives for greater productivity. There must not be room for complacency.

Some American companies have done well in Japan. They include IBM Japan and Coca Cola and their stories are told in Chapter 7. They have succeeded by being more "Japanese" than their Japanese competitors on some occasions and on others by insisting on American approaches. Yankee ingenuity and Americanism are still very much in evidence.

Why another book on Japanese management, you may ask. There is a sense of urgency I wish to share. Unless we are prepared to meet the Japanese challenge, the America we know may cease to be.

In 1976 and 1980, I tried for a seat in the U.S. Congress. I failed both times, but the experience left a long-lasting impression. Going through the hills and valleys of central Pennsylvania, I met many capable engineers and line workers who were out of work, all ready and willing, but without a position to fill. Some factories were practically empty with only a few machines humming. Dust on other machines remained undisturbed, along with cigarette butts on the floor from years past. In my mind was a scene from the meticulously clean Japanese factory floors where workers moved in orderly fashion. In the final analysis, productivity could not be measured in terms of machines and equipment. What really counted was the human factor. I felt a sense of sadness accompanied by a tinge of anger because no one seemed to care. There was neither the will nor the resolve to conquer the economic ills before us. In Japan this could not happen! Can we somehow find a way to reshape our economy by observing and perhaps following the Japanese examples?

To a varying degree, but without exception, those of us who have been exposed to Japan feel a sense of obligation to report to our fellow countrymen what is happening across the Pacific. Among specialists, perhaps I can now claim one of the longest exposures to Japan. I was born in 1928 in Taiwan, which was then a Japanese colony. My education was a vintage Japanese elite course, with middle and high school years spent at Taihoku Kotogakko, the island's only gateway to Japan's prewar imperial universities. Our teachers included Professor Inukai Takashi, recognized today as the foremost authority on the *Manyoshu*, Japan's oldest anthology of poems, and Professor Kito Saizo, the authority on *Renga*, fifteenth-century link verse. My Japanese education was rudely interrupted with the end of the war, and my college years were spent under the Chinese in Taiwan.

In 1950, I came to this country. At Columbia University my study of Japan continued; my doctoral dissertation was on the subject of Japan's entry into World War II. In 1960, the year I was naturalized, I began teaching at Bucknell University. My first assignment was in the broad area of Asian history but, since 1965, when the Center for Japanese Studies was established at Bucknell, my attention has been focused more and more on Japan.

In 1965, I had the privilege of meeting Prime Minister Sato Eisaku. By the time his term ended in 1972 I could call him my friend. He and other Japanese friends opened the door for me to the upper reaches of Japanese society, and that process has continued without interruption.

In 1972, Mr. Hasegawa Saiji left the presidency of the Jiji Press to establish an independent news-weekly company, Naigai News. My luncheon talk on U.S. policy in East Asia became a featured article in his paper, and I began writing for it fairly regularly. Mr. Hasegawa always believed in two-way communication between his writers and readers. One feature of his company was a series of monthly local meetings held across Japan. From time to time I was invited to address these meetings to explain America's political and economic practices, which appeared strange to the Japanese. These sessions in turn gave me unusual opportunities to meet Japanese civic and industrial leaders in a formal yet relaxed atmosphere.

Materials for this book come from three distinct sources: my own contacts described above, visits to 79 Japanese companies over an eight-year period, and extensive reading in Japanese of literature on Japanese companies.

The book's emphasis is of course on Japanese business practices. One underlying assumption, however, is that America is a "can-do" society. Coming from a culture where having live-in maids was taken for granted, when I first reached these shores in 1950, I was tremendously impressed to see U.S. corporate executives dirtying their hands to fix their cars, work on the garden or help their wives in the kitchen. In those dirty hands, I saw the very essence of America's work ethic. If our corporate executives will "dirty" their hands again alongside their line workers, we will witness the resurgence of American industry.

I owe the title of this book to my youngest son, Steve. He studied under the Associated Kyoto Program at Doshisha University in 1984-85. Before going to Japan, he asked me, "Dad, don't you think the strength of Japanese companies is in their ability to go ten yards for each four downs?" It was a good statement, showing how Japanese companies make their steady progression. Hence the football analogy of this book was born.

For the past decade, I have been teaching a course called "Business with Japan." From a modest beginning of eight or nine students, it now has about 185 students. One delightful aspect of this course is that somehow their parents also get involved. I receive questions from them about how Japanese companies behave and how to deal with them. If this book is "alive" and dealing with issues very much in the minds of American businessmen, I owe it to the questions raised both in and out of class sessions.

Some Bucknell football players have been in my classes, and once a capable quarterback was in the "Business with Japan" course. While they have not had a winning season on the playing field for several years, I hope they and their classmates and "teammates," in the broadest sense of that word, have continuous winning seasons in the real world as they practice the art of fumble-free management.

David J. Lu
Milton, Pennsylvania
March, 1987

A Note on Japanese Names

In Japan, the family name appears first. Thus the famed inventor of the Toyota production system is known in Japan as Ohno Taiichi, and not Taiichi Ohno as usually written in the West.

In *Inside Corporate Japan*, I have followed the Japanese practice. This is in part to make the representation of Japanese names uniform. A number of people from Japan's past, such as Toyotomi Hideyoshi (d. 1598), are cited in this book. Even in Western works, their names have always been given in the order they appear here, that is with their family names first. Consistency requires this practice. However, there is another consideration. If your name happens to be, say, Daniel Sutherland, you do not want your Japanese friends to call you Sutherland Daniel. Likewise, we must get into the habit of calling our Japanese friends by their correct names. It is common courtesy, and there is more on this subject in the appendix on business etiquette.

CHAPTER 1

Tokyo, Osaka and Nagoya

At 8:00 A.M., a bullet superexpress train, Hikari, with a double-deckered dining car and first-class compartments leaves Tokyo station. It arrives at Nagoya at 10:01 A.M., makes a two-minute stop, leaves for Kyoto, arriving there at 10:52 A.M., stops for one minute and then arrives in Osaka's new terminal at 11:00 A.M. On a clear day, the snow-capped Mt. Fuji is visible to the right. In the foreground, smokestacks of the industrial city of Fujisawa appear at one moment and then suddenly turn into the tea fields of Shizuoka. Traveling at a speed of more than one hundred miles an hour, the ride is deceptively smooth. In a private compartment, a dictaphone may be used and letters and memos written. It is a business express that provides comfort with efficiency.

A Tokyo businessman may either take this train to Osaka or choose from among nine earlier Hikari trains with the first leaving Tokyo at 6:00 A.M.; he may hold business conferences, attend a business luncheon and select one of the afternoon bullet trains for return to Tokyo. Of course, an Osaka businessman can do this in the reverse order. The bullet train has made the three cities of Tokyo, Osaka and Nagoya within commuting distance of each other.

On the surface, the three cities are very much alike. Each is serviced by excellent multiple subway systems and auxiliary and private rail lines, extending the reach of the city to the surrounding suburban areas. Department stores are within or near each of the terminals. Cabs lined up outside the stations also have a sameness about them. In their fast yet orderly movement, they represent the face of modern Japan.

Once the cab leaves the station, however, the pace quickly changes. In Osaka, the cab must travel through a stretch of expressway before entering the center of town. In Nagoya, the station is almost in the center. Yet the cab can travel quickly through avenues that are unusually broad for Japanese cities. In Tokyo, however, traffic congestion is the norm and not the exception. Even on the broad tree-lined avenues facing the Imperial Palace, movement can be painfully slow.

As the businessman leaves his cab, he hears language spoken with a distinct local flavor. The Kansai dialect, spoken in the Osaka area, engulfs the visitor like an octet with each player speaking in a crescendo. In Nagoya, each sentence ending is clearly punctuated, and — after a pause — another begins with a staccato. In contrast, the sound in Tokyo is less colorful. The standard language at times can sound effeminate, but it is Japan's counterpart of an Oxbridge accent — when spoken correctly, it always sounds polite.

The Kansai and Nagoya dialects are legacies of the feudal age that ended in 1867. The dialects have been continuously nurtured, however, through the Meiji-Taisho periods (1868-1926) to Showa, from the pre- to postwar eras up to the present. If a local businessman must transact business with someone from outside the region, the standard Tokyo dialect is used. If he meets his local colleague, they speak to each other in the local dialect. The local dialect is not taught to an outsider. One must be born into it. For two Kansai businessmen to be able to speak to one another in their common dialect is reaffirmation of their shared values and mutual trust. They may not always see things eye to eye, but in a pinch they come to each other's aid.

Everything being equal, with a contract to be given, Kansai businessmen will naturally prefer "one of our kind," meaning one who speaks the Kansai dialect and has roots firmly planted in the Kansai region. This exclusiveness in business practices, which American businessmen find objectionable and difficult to penetrate, is found time and again in Japan. The targets are not, however, American but Japanese firms from the differing regions.

In the United States, one tends to categorize Japanese businesses under the rubric of "Japan, Inc.," assuming that their operations are uniform and constantly guided by the Ministry of International Trade and Industry (MITI). This is far from the truth. In Japan as in the United States, company A can never be identical to company B. It is possible, however, to categorize Japanese companies into regional types that are nurtured by their common dialect and tradition. Companies in Osaka set goals and manage their affairs somewhat differently from those in Nagoya or Tokyo. Regional companies are aided by their "regional" banks and other regional industries. As they coalesce into a larger regional group with an enhanced sense of solidarity, they are better able to compete effectively in the domestic market. Once competitiveness is strengthened, it is extended to the overseas market.

This chapter studies the differing types of business practices in the three cities. For want of better terms, I shall name them the Kanto-type (Tokyo) industries, Nagoya-type industries and Kansai-type (Osaka) industries. We shall begin with the last one first.

KANSAI-TYPE INDUSTRIES

In 1982, the Nomura Research Institute selected 100 "excellent companies" (excluding insurance and financial institutions) from 960 whose stocks were traded on either the Tokyo or Osaka stock exchanges. Comprising less than 25 percent of companies listed on the two exchanges, Kansai companies represented 33 percent of those considered excellent. The criteria for selection were profitability, stability and growth potential.[1]

Profitability typifies Kansai companies more than any other criteria. Take, for example, Kyocera, which experienced a gross profit of ¥ 72,399 million against net sales of ¥ 28,325 million in 1985, at a pre-tax gross profit ratio of 25.6 percent.

World, a Kobe-based high fashion dress and suit maker, has 1,688 employees, and its stocks are yet to be traded on the exchanges. In 1983, it had a gross profit of ¥ 21,209 million. This figure compared favorably against the gross profit of ¥ 10,960 million realized by Reknown, the largest Tokyo-based fashion designer-manufacturer. The net sales for World in that year was ¥ 115,918 million, while that of Reknown was ¥ 210,431 million. When these figures are translated into the gross profit ratio, World's comes to 18.3 percent, and Reknown's, 5.2 percent. Reknown, incidentally, has 4,381 employees, and per employee, World far outdistances Reknown in profitability.

Examples like these abound. Why does this happen? It is not that Tokyo-based companies are fiscally irresponsible or unmindful of profit. It is rather a matter of emphasis. As Professor Yui Tsunehiko of Meiji University, who specializes in corporate histories, succinctly remarks, "Kansai companies put emphasis on profit while Kanto companies place value on the net sales."[2] To put it differently, Kansai companies, like their American counterparts, are quite concerned with the bottom line, while Tokyo-based companies are more interested in obtaining their market share.

Emphasizing market share works well in an expansive market. As long as the market is expanding, credit is easily obtained, and the company producing a certain commodity can benefit from an economy of scale. This is not to say that Kansai companies are not interested in market share. They are, but they are not willing to borrow just for the sake of expansion. If they borrow, they prefer to repay the loan as early as possible. Kansai businesses are thus more resilient, and when the economy is slow moving, they have fewer adjustments to make than their counterparts in Tokyo.

This emphasis on profitability and dislike for debt are expressions of Kansai-based industries' pragmatism. Aside from pragmatism, other characteristics of the Kansai industries include:

1. Ability to discern shifting winds of change and take appropriate action.

2. Willingness to experiment with the new and expand to new markets, even overseas.

3. Ability to make the government a willing business partner, without becoming subordinate to it.

4. Closeness to the customer.

5. Goal orientation or "future-mindedness."

Historical Background

The Osaka merchants' innovativeness and their ability to discern shifting winds of change have not come accidentally. Tradition and environment have been favorable to these developments.

The Kansai area was the political and economic center of the country for centuries, going back to the days of the founding of the nation. Kyoto became the imperial capital in 794 A.D. and retained that status until 1868. With the establishment of the Tokugawa Bakufu (Shogunate) in 1603, the de facto administrative center was moved to Edo, present-day Tokyo. The Emperor remained in Kyoto, however, maintaining the fiction that Kyoto was still the capital of the nation.

From 1467 to 1568, Japan was engulfed in a civil war. The battle cries of the competing *sengoku daimyo*, a new type of local authority who effectively controlled his domain, were to enter Kyoto and unify the country in the name of the Emperor. Highways and byways leading to Kyoto, which were all within the Kansai region, became the most fiercely fought battlegrounds. In order to survive, the Kansai merchants learned how to observe changes and collect information. A single mounted warrior charging to an unknown destination could be a portent for another battle. Decisions to buy, sell or store commodities were made quickly on the basis of this and other acquired information. That uncanny sense of observing the shifting winds of change has been transmitted through the generations.

Oda Nobunaga (1534-1582), the first general to unify the country, entered Kyoto in 1568. To solidify his power base, he established free market and guild-free zones. Merchants entering these zones were exempt from all levies and miscellaneous taxes assessed by local authorities, including feudal lords, temples and shrines. This was one of the very first steps taken toward creating a national economy. The first to benefit from this policy were the Kansai merchants.

Toyotomi Hideyoshi (1536-1598), Nobunaga's successor, erected a castle in Osaka in 1583. By then, Osaka was the administrative and commercial center of the nation. Foreign trade was encouraged by Hideyoshi through the grant of vermilion seals for ships sailing overseas. Osaka and the nearby port of Sakai prospered. With the death of Hideyoshi and the costly battle of Sekigahara (1600), which the Toyotomi forces lost, power shifted to the Tokugawa family and the administrative center was formally established in Edo in 1603. Loss of political power did not deter the Kansai region from growing economically, however. Throughout the Tokugawa period (1603-1867), Osaka retained its preeminent commercial position. Daimyo and samurai came to its merchant houses to exchange their rice revenue for cash. The Osaka merchants serviced the daimyo's debts and prospered while the daimyo and samurai became increasingly impoverished. A merchant-led culture was born. The glory of townspeople (*chonin*) was immortalized in the Kabuki and puppet plays of Chikamatsu Monzaemon (1653-1724) with Osaka as the focal point.

With a movement toward imperial restoration in the middle of the nineteenth century, Kyoto became a center of political intrigue. But Kyoto was to lose its position as the capital of the nation in 1868 with the advent of the Meiji Restoration. Tokyo became the new capital, but the Kansai region retained its dominant economic presence. The Tokyo area did not assert itself as the premier economic region of the nation until after its recovery from the Kanto earthquakes of 1923. Even then, Kansai produced more in heavy industries and chemicals. In the postwar era, especially after 1955 when Japan's economic recovery took off, the Kanto region's dominance became unmistakable. The Kansai region remained competitive in spirit, however. Tokyo was given the honor of hosting the 1964 Olympics, but the honor of hosting the first World's Fair in Asia went to Osaka in 1970, which incidentally was a profitable and successful one. Today Osaka can also boast one of the finest symphony orchestras in the world, its prestige often surpassing that of the many orchestras performing in Tokyo.

The Kanto region has developed much faster, and Osaka is no longer the second but the third largest city in the country. Yokohama has taken that distinction from Osaka. However, with the port city of Kobe within its environs, and the ancient city of Kyoto resurgent in modern industries, the Kansai region is still filled with vitality. Its leaders can still remember the days when Kansai was "number one" in various industrial categories. Their sense of regional solidarity is manifested in regional chambers of commerce and economic affairs meetings. They have not lost their spunk and, company for company, they still take pride in their ability to outperform their Kanto counterparts.

Inventiveness

There are seventy-four new types of business that have become well established in Japan since the end of the Second World War. Of these seventy-four, fifty-seven were created in the Kansai region. To name one, readers are familiar with Instant Ramen, or a Cup of Soup. Add hot water, let it steep for three minutes, and it becomes a nice cup of hot Japanese noodle soup. It is now available in supermarkets throughout the United States just as in Japan. This concept originated in Kansai.

So did the practice of *karaoke*, a concept similar to the music-minus-one record. A pre-taped orchestral accompaniment is available in a coffee shop or restaurant; a customer can come in and sing with the full accompaniment. He may be tone deaf and very shy but, for a brief moment, he is on stage acting a lot different than usual. It is an ego booster because a round of applause is sure to come from other customers. For tired businessmen, this has been a superb form of entertainment and today the practice is spreading across all four islands of Japan. *Karaoke* shops can be found in the streets of Taipei or other cities where Japanese businessmen frequent. Japanese civilization in the form of *karaoke* is now invading the Western Pacific!

In a more serious vein, the Temporary Center is an executive recruitment firm that also leases workers out for temporary assignments. In a Japan that prides itself on so-called lifetime employment, leasing out workers has previously been a taboo subject. But Osaka merchants are rational, practical and inventive. Their success in Osaka has led to the establishment of many Temporary Center branches across the country, with a significant presence in Tokyo.

Overseas Commitment

Proportionately there are more Kansai-related firms doing business in the United States than from other regions. Just to name a few, Matsushita, Sanyo, Sumitomo, Sanwa, Ito Chu, Marubeni, Kanebo, Kyocera and Suntory are all Kansai-based companies. They came to the United States earlier than most and also advertise more heavily. Sasakawa Express, another Kyoto-based company, is a major sponsor of CNN's Saturday night series called "This Week in Japan."

The Osaka merchants' penchant for overseas expansion is well represented by Iue Toshio, who named his fledgling company

Sanyo, meaning three oceans. This forty-four-year-old entrepreneur's idea was to sell his products all over the world, across the three oceans. But on February 1, 1947, when he established his company, he had a total of fifteen employees, and his sole product was a battery-operated bicycle lamp.

Then there is Takara Belmont, a barber and dental chair concern. It was established in 1921 as a small forging factory in Osaka by Yoshikawa Hidenobu, then twenty-two. In 1954, Yoshikawa set foot on U.S. soil for the first time, having placed a barber chair on exhibit in an international exposition held in Seattle. His previous overseas sales experience consisted of selling a few barber chairs in pre-World War II China, but he was determined to conquer the American market. He had nothing going for him except his resolve, and his slogan was "Do not think of today's merchandise; think about something that can be sold tomorrow."

At this time a barber chair made by Koken of St. Louis was sold at a premium in Japan. Undaunted, Yoshikawa established an American subsidiary in 1957 and a British subsidiary in 1959. By the time of his death in 1983, there were seventeen major subsidiaries worldwide, and in 1969 Takara absorbed Koken of St. Louis. In this case the smaller absorbed the larger, and Takara now controls close to 100 percent of barber chair sales in the United States. Near the end of his life, Yoshikawa devoted his full energy to developing Brazil. Aside from establishing successful barber and dental chair operations there, he wanted Brazil to become a supplier of agricultural products and new energy sources for Japan. When asked why, his response was disarmingly simple: "The world is one, isn't it?"[3] And this came from a man who was a grade school dropout and started working at the age of ten to support his family.

Partnership with the Government

Takara Belmont entered the American market earlier than

almost any other Japanese company. When it encountered legal problems, the Japanese embassy in Washington provided expert guidance. At the time it purchased Koken, the company was subjected to an antitrust investigation, and again, the Japanese embassy helped Takara find an American law firm to represent it. In spite of all the assistance it received, Takara's relationship with the Japanese government has never been one binding a supplicant to a superior authority. If anything, it can be described as that binding partners joined in a common cause of promoting Japanese industry overseas. As one of Takara's executives expresses it, "We are grateful for the help we received. At the same time, what we did has helped others. By helping us enter the American market, the embassy has acquired the experience necessary to help other Japanese companies."

In the feudal days, Osaka merchants knew that the daimyo, no matter how powerful, were at their mercy when it came to the matter of finance. The so-called stratification of status always placed the samurai class at the top and merchants at the bottom, but the former needed the services of the latter. In reality, the official doctrine was set aside and the two classes complemented each other in performing their respective obligations. The sense of partnership took hold much more firmly in the Kansai region than any other place. The city of Osaka, for example, was governed directly by the Tokugawa Bakufu. There was no daimyo as overlord and no coteries of Confucian scholars to pontificate on the virtue of perpetual separation of the classes. When daimyo sought financial and other services from the merchants, they became outsiders seeking the favors of insiders — merchants who were more sophisticated in the ways of the world. That sense of partnership and sharing of power still survives to this day in Kansai.

JETRO is a familiar name for people doing business with Japan. It stands for Japan External Trade Organization, which has offices in major cities around the world. Initially it was started as an agency to promote Japan's exports, but lately it has been engaged more and more in aiding foreign business firms planning to enter the Japanese market. The first JETRO office was opened in Osaka on February 18, 1951. The idea for such an organization came from trade associations in Osaka. Technically JETRO is a "corporation having a special status," meaning that the government, in this case MITI, is its main financial sponsor. Its personnel are interchangeable with other governmental officials, but it is not a governmental bureau and is less formal and bureaucratic. It can serve effectively as a vehicle for cooperation between the private and public sectors. It is a typical Kansai way of doing business.

In dealing with governmental agencies, the Kansai merchants stress balance. When this balance is not carefully observed, trouble can ensue. In 1971, the Japanese government agreed to impose voluntary quotas on textile exports to the United States. The task of informing the textile industry and enforcing the quotas fell on the shoulders of the Minister of International Trade and Industry, Miyazawa Kiichi. Unlike the automobile quotas imposed in later years, quotas on textiles were difficult to enforce. There were simply too many companies engaged in textiles, and assignment of quotas could not satisfy everyone. Past records of sales in the United States were not the best guide in this volatile market. Aside from a sense of frustration and the knowledge that they were sacrificed for the sake of the return of Okinawa promised for 1972, the textile traders, who were concentrated in Kansai, resented the high-handedness of the government.[4] The voluntary quota was a political and economic failure.

Closeness to the Customer

The Kansai industries' vitality and independence are supported by another of their virtues — being close to their customers. In Kansai, this closeness is expressed in a traditional term, *maedare seishin*, which evokes a picture of an apron-clad lad serving as an apprentice in a commercial establishment.

Translated into modern language, it means that manufacturers and vendors alike must serve their customers and know their needs accurately at all times.

Back in 1972, Matsushita introduced an electric range with an oven, but its sales never took off. Japanese homemakers were satisfied with their old burners and found very little use for the oven. Baking at home was still a novel concept. Matsushita's answer was to organize OSPA troops, which stood for "Oven Sales Promotion Attackers." Each group consisted of nine members, four men and five women, who crisscrossed the country giving cooking and baking lessons. All members were taught to observe the reactions of the customers while they served as short order cooks and bakers demonstrating the new product. Having men demonstrate the new oven served two purposes. First, their presence aroused curiosity among housewives, who were the customers the company wanted to impress. Second, through the demonstration tours, these men became good cooks and bakers and unwittingly shared a common experience with their customers. That common experience was useful when they were on the factory floor to produce or on the tour to sell the appliances. The *maedare seishin* always calls for this kind of close identification with the customer.

In speaking of the spirit of service to the customer, one can never forget the management genius Kobayashi Ichizo (1873-1957). Founder of the Hankyu Rail Lines, he sold housing sites along his rail lines to create more customers for the lines. He was the originator of the terminal department store concept. At railway terminals, department stores were to be built with movie theaters, children's amusement centers, restaurants and even outdoor beer gardens. His rail lines were profitable during the morning and evening rush hours, but not during the day. With the establishment of a terminal department store, housewives could shop at leisure while their husbands were at work, and their use of trains during the non-rush hours brought profit to the company. Kobayashi was able to do these things because he always had his ears attuned to customer needs, not forgetting the women at home. For men, incidentally, he created the Takarazuka Girls' Follies at the opposite end of his rail lines, where a department store would not have been economically justifiable at that time.

Hanshin Electric Railway is a competitor of Hankyu, operating a rail line linking Osaka with Kobe. Among other things, it owns a baseball franchise, the Hanshin Tigers, and nowhere else could one find the symbiosis of Kansai merchants with their customers better manifested than when that team won the national championship in the fall of 1985. The Hanshin Department Store immediately went on a sales spree, "doing one better" what the Seibu Department Store did in previous years when its team won. There was a joy of victory against the archrival and the joy of humiliating the Tokyo region. Even more impressive than Hanshin's sales spree were the celebrations sponsored by small shopkeepers. They had their own bargain sales to conduct, including five-cents-a-cup coffee and all-the-beer-you-can-drink celebrations. One of the coffee shop owners remarked on a national TV network, "Oh boy, I lost so much money with those five-cent cups of coffee and I have never had so much fun in my entire life!" Yet at heart he was also a calculating Osaka merchant. That TV spot, which he could never purchase on his own at prime time, would insure a lot more customers from the next day on.

Future-mindedness

"I have always been concerned how Japan is going to be and how the world is going to be in the future," says Matsushita Konosuke. "It is not a scholarly prediction. I simply perceive of the changes intuitively and think of the future.... The issue, however, is this," he continues. "In order for Japan to benefit from world prosperity in the twenty-first century, what must Matsushita Electric Industrial Company do?"[5]

These words were spoken by a man who was born in 1894.

This future-mindedness is typical of many corporate executives in Kansai and in Japan as a whole. By looking toward the future, a company also becomes goal oriented. Corporate objectives are clearly articulated that give support in turn to the established corporate philosophy. This ability to look to the future is a subject important enough to be treated fully in another chapter. (See Chapter 6).

NAGOYA - TYPE INDUSTRIES

In 1610, Tokugawa Ieyasu (1542-1616) ordered that a castle be erected in Nagoya and enfeoffed his son Yoshinao in the province of Owari, which corresponds to the western part of the present-day Aichi prefecture. Nagoya was located on the Tokaido, the most important east-west highway linking Edo (Tokyo) with Kyoto. Through an auxiliary highway, Nagoya was also linked to the Nakasendo, another major east-west thoroughfare. It was Ieyasu's desire that his son guard this castle against attack from potential enemies from the west. As long as Nagoya was secure, approaches to Edo would remain protected.

As an important castle town, Nagoya prospered economically, but it could never match the exuberance of Osaka or the prosperity of Edo. In the middle of the eighteenth century, the population of Edo was estimated at over one million, Kyoto at about half a million and Osaka at 400,000. In contrast, Nagoya had perhaps only 63,000 inhabitants. To compensate for the smallness of their own territory and population, Nagoya merchants travelled far and wide in other areas. They became itinerant peddlers, always working hard to learn skills from others, and were never given to temptations of luxury afforded by Edo and Osaka. People from these urban centers might call them peasants, but Nagoya merchants knew their own business well. They knew how to secure their own holdings, and protect their "own castle."

Tradition has a way of surviving through the ages. Ishida Taizo became president of Toyota Motors in 1950 and remained in that position until 1961. He is credited with Toyota's resurgence. His famous slogan for the company was: "Let us protect our own castle with our own hands." It touched responsive chords among Toyota employees who were mostly from Aichi.

Today, the fifty kilometer radius around Nagoya commands a population of about eight million, which is about one-half the size of a similar area in Osaka, and two-sevenths the size of the one in Tokyo. The port of Nagoya follows Yokohama and Kobe respectively in the amount of cargo carried for exports. They are third, not first or second, but they are more intensely dedicated to their work. Paraphrasing an American advertising slogan, "We are third, and we try even harder," describes Nagoya well.

Toyota, Noritake and Brothers are among the companies that originated in this region. They have come through adversity to gain their present prominence. There are also the lesser known Okuma and Yamazaki iron works that are making an impressive inroad in the machine tool field in the United States.

Basic attitudes are difficult to change, however. The lifestyle of Nagoya merchants is more spartan, and so is the appearance of the city. Nagoya does not have its Ginza, Roppongi or Dotonbori — Japan's answers to the Piccadilly Circus or Champs Elysees. Such honor is reserved exclusively for Tokyo and Osaka. Nor is the city known for its symphonies or theaters. The basic approach is no-nonsense, getting on with business — an approach that is pragmatic and rational to the core.

In Nagoya, to be called "stingy" (*kechi kechi*) can be a badge of honor. "Do not spend money unless it is absolutely necessary" — and the standards Nagoya people impose on themselves can be rather stringent. According to one story a wealthy executive insisted that all of his sons and employees retain envelopes received, steam them, turn them over, repaste and reuse them. It was not that he could ill afford new envelopes, but why waste those perfectly reusable ones! He was not worried about the adverse corporate image this little action might have created.

The practice of stinginess is not confined to this and other unknown companies. Even a giant like Toyota does not mind cultivating an image of being stingy. The company has an attractive olympic-size stadium and actively sponsors athletic meets for its employees. Preparation was underway for Toyota Olympics in the spring of 1977 when an outside contractor submitted an estimate of ¥1.7 million to lime the 400-meter, eight-course track. Toyota decided to reject the estimate and called in its car paint section to lime the entire track. It completed the same job with a mere ¥60,000! The ¥1.7 million estimate submitted was not out of line, and to a company like Toyota it was a piddling sum. If there can be a saving, however, there must be a saving! This dedication to stinginess provided fertile soil for the development of the Toyota production system.

Rationalism — Dedication to Eliminating Waste

Normally we perceive the Toyota production system as supported by the just-in-time system and the kanban (signpost) system. This perception is not wrong, but we must not forget that the two systems are merely a means for attaining the ultimate goal of total elimination of waste. As Ohno Taiichi, former executive vice president of Toyota and inventor of the just-in-time system, remarks: "It's a crime to overproduce." Aside from the waste arising from overproduction, there are other categories of wastes, such as those arising from time on hand, transporting, processing itself, unnecessary stock on hand, unnecessary motion and producing defects. The Toyota system is designed to eliminate all of these wastes from its manufacturing process. Man-hour reduction becomes possible only after these categories of waste (*muda*) are eliminated, along with unevenness (*mura*) and unreasonableness (*muri*).

In promoting the introduction of its just-in-time system, Toyota does not demand that new machines be installed. If old machines can be fixed to do the job, that is fine. Or if workers can be reassigned to bring about man-hour reduction, that is also fine. A new machine can be expensive and, of course, "no unnecessary money must be spent." The Toyota production system and Nagoya's stinginess are not strangers.

Stretching this observation a little further, Nagoya can provide a most unusual mixture of the old and new. In Tokyo, the Imperial Palace, which is the old Edo Castle, has an outer moat that is always filled with water. It provides a nostalgic view of the past that is especially attractive when the cherry blossoms are in full bloom. The Nagoya Castle also has an outer moat but without water. It is not abandoned but turned into a railway track on which Meitetsu (Nagoya Railroad) operates one of its suburban lines. Meitetsu is one of the fourteen major privately owned railway companies. It operates 544 kilometers (338 miles) of rail lines, making it the second largest railroad company in terms of the length of its lines. Its public-spiritedness is demonstrated by its founding of the Meiji Village, which contains a large number of fully restored buildings designated as important cultural treasures from the Meiji period. For example, the old Imperial Hotel, which withstood the great Kanto earthquake of 1923 and made its designer Frank Lloyd Wright world famous, is partially restored there. It was rebuilt brick by brick, using the material carefully disassembled at its original site. The village also contains the house in which the famed author Natsume Soseki (1867-1916) wrote his first novel, I Am a Cat. The village has been a favorite destination for field trips but so far is a money-losing proposition.

When it comes to business, however, Meitetsu is highly competitive. When its lines come into direct competition against the lines of the National Railways, it utilizes the sleek modern-looking passenger trains. In the outer moat suburban line, there is no competition and vintage cars are used. On a hot summer day, passengers sweat profusely without the benefit of air conditioning. Sometimes there may be an insect bite or two, but it is good management, Nagoya style.

Management by Wandering Around

Management by walking around and stinginess may not be two sides of the same coin precisely, but they share one feature in common — dedication to the total elimination of waste. To succeed requires a trained manager with minimal interference from the corporate staff. It presupposes that corporate staff be lean and always willing to engage in a man-hour reduction movement of its own. It is no wonder successful examples of management by wandering around can be found most frequently in the Nagoya area.

Toyoda Gosei is one of the Toyota group companies. It produces car parts, rubber and plastic products and related household products. Its president, Nemoto Masao, is an expert on total quality control who came to Toyoda Gosei after serving as a managing director of Toyota. Nemoto's favorite management method is to be close to his workers and to converse with them as frequently as time permits. A typical day at Toyoda Gosei may find Nemoto on the floor of one of its manufacturing plants accompanied by the plant manager or assistant manager. As they wander around, a group of two or three workers will stop them. "Mr. President, may we have a word with you?" A few minutes later, the same scene will be repeated by another group and then by yet another. The two-way conversation rarely lasts more than three minutes, but procedures to be altered, materials to be inspected and the like can be effectively discussed. An engineer by training, Nemoto becomes a teacher in these conversations.[6]

This scene is not confined to Toyoda Gosei. At Amita, a fishnet-making machine manufacturer located in Toyohashi (the second largest city in the Aichi prefecture to the east of Nagoya), president Yamamoto Tei can be found wandering around his factory floor and business offices. He knows what is going on in his company at all times. His fishnet-making machine is exported to over fifty countries around the world, and Yamamoto keeps up with full details concerning each transaction, including some custom-made parts needed for new customers. An effective wandering-around style of management eliminates the need for unnecessary paperwork and permits quicker decision making. This is one of the hallmarks of Nagoya-style management.

KANTO-TYPE INDUSTRIES

Geographically, the Kanto region consists of the Tokyo metropolitan district and six other prefectures of Ibaraki, Tochigi, Gumma, Saitama, Chiba and Kanagawa. For the purpose of this book, however, the term is narrowly defined to include only Tokyo and the three prefectures of Kanagawa, Saitama and Chiba. This area, according to the last national census completed on October 1, 1985, has a total population of 30,271,701. It represents almost exactly 25 percent of Japan's total population of 121,047,196.

This region has three of Japan's ten most populated cities, Tokyo, Yokohama and Kawasaki. The outlying areas of Kanagawa, Saitama and Chiba have been turned into bedroom communities for Tokyo. Through the act of commuting to school and work, most of the region's population shares the common Tokyo experience.

Unlike the Kansai region where Osaka, Kyoto and Kobe still maintain their distinctiveness, in the Kanto region, such distinction among cities has become blurred. Yokohama is now larger than Osaka, but taking a train from Tokyo to Yokohama, one does not know where one city ends and another begins. In between is Kawasaki, with a population of over one million, but one can pass it without even noticing.

If major cities lack their own separate identities, that fact is compensated by the existence of distinct centers developed within the metropolitan region. In Shinjuku, now an auxiliary metropolitan center, with a number of fifty-story buildings housing major corporations and smaller enterprises.

Ikebukuro has its shopping and office complex named Sunshine City and a world trade center. In Hamamatsucho, another world trade building serves as the terminus for a monorail train to Haneda airport. The new bullet trains to Morioka to the north and Niigata on the Japan Sea coast leave from Ueno, the traditional gateway to the north. Modern in some areas, Ueno still retains the charm of prewar Tokyo, with some of its buildings harking back to the Edo period. The old neighborhood is alive and well in Ueno. These centers, Shinjuku, Ikebukuro, Hamamatsucho and Ueno, incidentally, are linked by the Yamanote line that circles Tokyo.

Within Tokyo proper there are other centers like Asakusa with its Kannon (Goddess of Mercy) Temple as the focal point. Asakusa is where downtown people — successors to the Edo period's *chonin* or townspeople — congregate. There is Ginza with many modern department stores, but tradition lurks in unexpected places. For instance, Akihabara is known for its endless rows of electronics shops offering anything from computer chips to the latest VCRs at bargain basement prices. Its products make Akihabara the most modern emporium, but the concept of bunching together shops in the same trade originated in the late sixteenth century.

In 1590, Tokugawa Ieyasu began building a new castle town on the site of a former fishing village. It had been developed earlier by Ota Dokan in 1457, but not in the scale envisioned by Ieyasu. The latter's answer was to move merchants and artisans en masse from Mikawa, his former fief, to Edo. All the trades were represented; even dollmakers were assigned an exclusive district. Unwittingly, Ieyasu created a system in which merchants in the same trade competed fiercely in their own neighborhood but learned to cooperate with each other in dealing with the authorities. That tradition survives in Japan today.

With the expansion of population in the Kanto region, smaller cities have been integrated generally into the metropolitan area through various rapid transit networks. Cities such as Hachijoji, Tachikawa, Omiya, Urawa, Chiba, Tsuchiura,

Tsukuba and Fujisawa, however, have been able to maintain their identities as distinct centers. Like Ikebukuro or Ueno, they are modern counterparts of the Greek agora, marketplaces where people congregate for economic and political purposes.

Kanto-type industries are harder to categorize because of their sheer number. Here are some forced generalizations which are by no means complete:

1. In the trendy, youth-oriented innovative enterprises, the Kanto region will remain dominant. The population in the region is predominantly young. When the mean value for each age group is set at fifty, the deviation value for the fifteen to twenty-four-year-old group in Tokyo is registered at 84.7, and that of Kanagawa at 60.64.

2. Tokyo is already the undisputed information center of the nation and INS (information network system) and other futuristic enterprises will have the best chance of success in this region. Mitaka, a city to the west of Tokyo proper, already has an INS program installed on an experimental basis.

3. The Kanto region has a number of superb research facilities, including those maintained by the government in Tsukuba. In the high-tech fields, including development of the fifth generation of computers, the Kanto region will remain competitive with any other region in the world. In Kanto, Japanese computer and electronics firms have the advantage of geographical concentration with different sectors supporting each other.

4. Tokyo is fast emerging as the second most important financial market in the world. The liberalization of the financial and stock markets begun in 1984 is irreversible.

5. There is a trend toward service-oriented industries, for which Tokyo will lead the way.

6. In manufacturing, the future is not as bright for the Kanto region as for the rest of the country. The most modern steel plant in the nation, Nippon Kokan's Ohgishima plant, is operated only at about half capacity. Shops in Kawasaki, subcontracted by firms like Isuzu, may operate at full capacity, but their

antiquated facilities suggest that their competitive days may be numbered.

The Kanto region's ability to invest in new equipment and facilities is not as promising as in other regions. There is the perennial problem of high land prices and space is limited at any price. Labor relations, not a serious issue in other regions, can be a problem in Kanto. When all costs are considered, the manufacturing sector in Kanto may find that it is no longer competitive with other regions, including the United States.

7. The Kanto business community's working relations with the government will remain cordial and much closer than in the rest of the country. Their relations are further cemented by college ties and the ability to informally meet with each other fairly often. The business community is generally willing to take administrative guidance from the bureaucrats. They are also happy to accept former bureaucrats as directors of their companies in a phenomenon known as *amakudari*, or descending from heaven. In return, the business community receives access and favorable considerations. Sometimes, however, the roles may be reversed. For example, business interests continue to pressure the government to undertake some administrative reform measures by Doko Toshio, the octogenarian former president of the Keidanren (Federation of Economic Associations).

Sony provides a good illustration for some points made in the observation above. Its Walkman cassette player was successful because Sony discerned the likes and dislikes of young people.[7] It created demands where none existed before. Its technological breakthroughs, from the first tape recorder in Japan, to Trinitron, Beta VCRs and compact disc players, have always drawn on the technical expertise available in the Kanto region. Relations with the government have remained cordial. Ibuka Masaru, one of the Sony founders and its honorary chairman, has served on a number of government advisory committees, and so has Morita Akio, another founder and the present chairman. Morita has also served a term as Japan's representative in the so-called wisemen's group, a U.S.-Japan Advisory Commission established by the two governments to defuse some of the knotty problems surrounding trade friction.

Sony is well known in the United States for its technology. Less known is its ability to cultivate good relations with the government, an equally important factor in its success. Ibuka is a son-in-law of Maeda Tamon, a former Minister of Education. When Sony was first established, Maeda was asked to be its first president, providing the fledgling company with respectability. Maeda in turn asked Tajima Michiji, a college friend of his, to serve on the board of directors. Tajima was a noted banker and his career included a long term of distinguished service as Grand Steward of the Imperial Household Agency. It was Tajima who persuaded Their Majesties to visit Sony on more than one occasion.

Ibuka can still recall vividly the day when they first announced the transistorized TV. The Emperor and Empress were visiting Sony's factory, accompanied by many attendants from whose view the new product should be hidden before its formal introduction. Waiting until Their Majesties withdrew to a private room with only the Governor of Tokyo, the Grand Chamberlain, the Mistress of Robes and Mr. Morita present, Ibuka carefully unwrapped the five-inch TV. The Emperor's transfixed eyes said it all. The introduction, of course, was a success and became an important media event as well.

Like other Tokyo industries, Sony tends to be more conscious of its public image than its counterparts in Kansai and Nagoya. At EXPO/85, the science and technology fair held in Tsukuba, Sony created the largest outdoor screen in the world. In contrast, Sharp declined to have its own pavilion. Sharp was the same company that in 1970, when EXPO/70 was held at its own doorstep in Osaka, refused to have a pavilion. It spent an equivalent amount building a semiconductor factory. The difference in style is strikingly evident.

REFLECTIONS

What do all of the above mean to America? Can the American government and businessman act differently vis-à-vis Japan?

First, we must eliminate from our thinking the idea that there is a Japan, Inc., with phalanxes of invaders ready to move anywhere in the world at MITI's command. Tokyo businessmen behave quite differently from their counterparts in Osaka. The government's administrative guidance, readily obeyed in Tokyo, may not be accepted in Osaka or Nagoya. Regional differences are significant, and within the same region, companies differ from one another. American companies that plan to enter the Japanese market, or that feel threatened by the Japanese companies' presence in the United States, must study their competition case by case and devise appropriate countermeasures. An appeal to the U.S. or Japanese government for redress is often an exercise in futility, since Japan Inc. is more facade than reality, and even the Japanese government lacks adequate enforcement powers.

When an American company plans to enter Japan, it is not advisable to choose the Tokyo market automatically. The Kanto region is too complex and the initial cost of establishing a presence can be prohibitive. Instead, the company may wish to consider Kansai or Nagoya, which are more manageable. When one of these regions proves too difficult to enter, then test marketing in other regional cities such as Sendai, Hiroshima or Okayama may be the answer.

Japanese companies that have entered or are entering the American market are formidable competitors. They are tough because they are well trained in their domestic market before coming to the U.S. — first in their respective regional markets and then in their national market. True, there are many failures in Japan and, in fact, their bankruptcy rate for medium and small sized companies is higher than that for the United States. When they survive their own version of trial by fire, however, they are ready to meet their next challenge vigorously, often catching their opponents unaware.

The vigorous regional markets, such as Kanto, Kansai and Nagoya, have given Japanese companies entering the United States added competitive advantages. In earlier days when things were not going smoothly, Matsushita used to appeal to regional pride, asking suppliers to lower the cost and distributors to pay a premium for its yet-to-be-proven products. Most suppliers and distributors are obliged to help a local company. This idea of "protecting our own against others" in domestic competition, when translated into the international scene, becomes one of "protecting the interest of Japanese companies against that of foreign companies." Even if fierce competitors at home, they would be quite willing to assist one another in a foreign environment. If a sports analogy can be used, let us assume that a "world series" game is to be played between an American champion team and a Japanese champion, say the Seibu Lions. The American team comes to the stadium ready to face Seibu. What it sees on the mound, however, is Japan's strike-out king from the rival Hankyu Tigers, with the best hitters from the Yomiuri Giants and Hiroshima Carps also on the team. The Japanese have engaged in the post-season trade, forgetting their erstwhile rivalries to create a super-team just for this encounter. Befuddled, the odds-on-favorite American team loses the game.

With the entry of highly competitive and successful Japanese companies in the arena, the world economy cannot be the same. It is an entirely new ball game with a new set of rules. To cope with it, American companies must revise their strategies.

CHAPTER 2

Organizing for
Fumble-Free Teamwork

I n Japan an old saying enjoins young people not to "let the work of creating a great mound fail for lack of one basket full of soil" (*senjin no ko o ikki ni kaku*). To do so is like being one foot from the goal line and fumbling the ball, negating the ninety-nine-yard drive that would have placed the team on top. In recent years, in economic competition, Japanese companies have sustained their drives, while U.S. companies have conceded defeat — not be cause the latter have been less capable, but because they have simply fumbled the ball too often. In contrast, Japanese companies seldom fumble or allow their opponents to intercept. Through fierce competition at home and overseas, they have acquired the art of fumble-free management.

The key to Japanese success has been dedication to teamwork and desire to promote human resources (*jinzai*). Many American observers as well as their Japanese counterparts ascribe Japanese success to cultural factors. For example, Americans cite the fact that living in limited space, the Japanese people have learned to work together closely and harmoniously. A generalization of this type, however, immediately brings out its own inherent flaws. If this assumption were accepted at face value, how could one explain the cutthroat competition existing among Japanese children to enter the best secondary school, in order to one day obtain admission to Tokyo University? There is nothing harmonious about the excessive zeal in the competition for limited spaces in prestigious universities. In fact, one can argue just as strongly that teamwork exists in Japanese companies in spite of Japanese proclivities to be otherwise.

Teamwork is certainly not a uniquely Japanese cultural attribute. Joe Paterno, Penn State's head football coach and 1986 recipient of the Bear Bryant award for best coach and Sports Illustrated's sportsman of the year award, is a modest man. That year, his team ranked number two in the nation after Miami. He is always generous in his praise for the opposing team's players. In recent years, his own team has not produced Heisman trophy winners or great stars of first-draft-choice caliber. In 1982, however, his team won against the favored Georgia team for the national championship and repeated the same feat in 1987 against Miami. In both instances, the opposing teams had Heisman trophy recipients leading their offensive units.

Joe Paterno's winning formula is deceptively simple. He relies on teamwork and insists that academic quality not be sacrificed. In Japan that would translate into promoting *jinzai* or human resources.

Like Joe Paterno, Japanese companies have discovered that combining teamwork and enhancement of human resources creates a winning formula. They have come to this conclusion because the formula works, not because it is part of the Japanese tradition. If anything, Japan's past has been dotted with the names of great masters — whether in tea ceremony, swordmaking or amassing wealth — who were known for their individual accomplishments and not for their skills in teamwork. Similarly, in combat the term *ikkiuchi* means one-to-one encounter, and traditionally an individual act of valor was highly praised.

The Japanese have discovered the art of teamwork slowly. While the date may not be precise, only around 1955 did Japanese companies begin offering so-called lifetime employment to their employees, inculcating in them the desire to serve the company effectively through teamwork. This was when Japanese recovery was about to take off and labor shortages began to be manifested.

A CAREER PATH

Training an employee to become an effective team player begins on the very first day of employment. This can be demonstrated through the career path of a typical white-collar worker we shall call Hiroki.

Hiroki is twenty-two and a graduate of a national university. He was referred to the company by his professor and successfully passed the prescribed entrance examination. In April, shortly after his graduation from college, he entered the company. After a reception in the company, which included a speech by the company president, he was sent to a Zen temple where the group of new management trainees dined together, slept in the same dormitory, swept the garden together, and formed task forces to attend to kitchen duties and clean bathrooms alternately. When this was over he was assigned to Section A.

In Japanese companies, sections constitute the basic building blocks. At the new section, Hiroki is the only one from his training group, but he is not alone and isolated. His on-the-job training is about to begin.

The day for Section A officially begins with a fifteen-minute talk by the section chief. It is a combination of pep talk, identifying targets for the day and briefings on company events. The chief assigns an employee to train Hiroki on a one-to-one basis. After a month or so when Hiroki masters everything taught by that employee, another is assigned to train him. In the meantime, Hiroki may assist in the work of these employees. After a year in this section of about fifteen members, Hiroki knows everyone's work thoroughly. This experience is intended to train him as a generalist who knows every aspect of the work performed in the section.

Unlike his counterparts in the United States, Hiroki's progress in the Japanese corporate ladder is a slow one. He does not receive promotion in rank until seven or eight years after his entry into the company. He becomes a *kakaricho* or a subsection chief. It is a modest title, but in the eyes of the company he has clearly made the mark. After two or three years, he may be moved laterally to another subsection either within his own section or in another. Job rotation begins at this point and takes place every two or three years. It is intended to train Hiroki to know all aspects of the activities in his division. If Hiroki is in a bank, a trading company or any other company with a significant foreign presence, he may even be given a tour of duty overseas.

If everything goes well, in his late thirties, Hiroki will be appointed to the position of *kacho*, or section chief. He may remain there for a number of years or receive another round of job rotation to make him more conversant with the company's varied activities. The title of *bucho*, or division manager, comes when Hiroki is in his late forties. At the age of fifty-two or fifty-three, Hiroki begins to fret over his own job performance. No matter how well he may have done, he knows that he must retire at age fifty-five (sixty in some companies), unless he is appointed a company director. Once he becomes a director, mandatory retirement no longer applies and he can remain with the company. If he is lucky he may even become the company president.

The organizational chart of the company where Hiroki works may appear as follows:

Chairman (*Kaicho*)
President (*Shacho*)
Vice-President (*Fuku Shacho*)
Senior Executive Director (*Semmu Torishimariyaku*)
Managing Director (*Jomu Torishimariyaku*)
Director (*Torishimariyaku*)
Division Manager (*Bucho*)
Deputy Division Manager (*Bucho Dairi*)
Section Chief (*Kacho*)
Deputy Section Chief (*Kacho Dairi*)
Subsection Chief (*Kakaricho*)
Regular Employees (*Shain*)

As Hiroki's example demonstrates, promotion is typically slow in Japanese companies. Job rotation is practiced frequently to train employees and create a sense of cohesiveness in the company. Along with job rotation, continuous on-the-job training is carried out from the first day at work until the day of retirement. The layers separating ordinary company employees and line workers from top management are far fewer in Japan than in the United States, which contributes to the Japanese companies' ability for faster decision making and effective implementation.

Slow Promotion

A Japanese bank employee carries a *meishi* (business card) with his name printed on both sides of the card, one side in English and the other in Japanese. On the Japanese side, his title is given as a *kacho* or chief of a certain section, but on the other side, it is printed as vice-president in charge of a certain section. In this he is not trying to overstate his position to his foreign friends. To reach the position of *kacho*, however, he has worked for fifteen years and has a vast responsibility in his bank. In America his counterpart may be called a senior vice-president. The plethora of titles American banks have invented — assistant vice-president, vice-president, senior vice-president, executive vice-president, senior executive vice-president, and so forth — answers the current generation's desire for rewards and status. In not succumbing to this temptation, Japanese banks and companies are making a clear-cut statement that the practice of slow promotion is there to stay in their respective organizations.

Slow promotion in title has several advantages. It reduces internal conflict. Too often in America, differences in the amount of bonuses, title and use of a company car have been sources of endless conflict within the same organization. It is built into the American system that individuals compete against each other fiercely. Infighting has almost been part of the American tradition. The Japanese system, in contrast, is designed to foster teamwork, if not complete harmony.

By the time Hiroki is promoted to the position of *kakaricho*, seven or eight years have elapsed. By then Hiroki has worked with everyone in the section, having been trained by some and in turn having trained others. His work habits and personality are well known to his superiors, colleagues and those expected to work under him. In those seven or eight years he has done a number of things that have brought credit to his entire section. If he is promoted to this position ahead of his "class," his colleagues will understand it clearly and without resentment. Those working under him will seek his help eagerly.

Hiroki attains his new position not through infighting but through active support of others. His many supervisors have had time to observe him and his initial step toward middle management comes with their joint blessings. His job performance, of course, has been weighed.

More important than the ability to perform, however, is his personality. Questions like "Does he get along well with others?" and "Is he helpful to other employees?" are asked. Then there is the question of *seijitsusa* or *seijitsusei*. The term is loosely translated as "sincerity." It may test the person's reliability, dedication to his job and loyalty to the company. It is not a quantifiable concept and he is judged on a feeling of trustworthiness. His current and former supervisors may meet and informally discuss his promotion, but seldom is a rating sheet used. By the time his new position is announced, no one questions the wisdom of his appointment.

One additional factor easing Hiroki's entry into the ranks of middle management is the seniority wage system (*nenko joretsu*) in determining salaries and wages. Assuming that Hiroki is the first one in his "class" of college graduates to attain a managerial position, the salary he receives will remain essentially the same as that of his "classmates" who entered the company the same year. Thus resentment from his peers with similar educational backgrounds will be far less than in the United States.

Job Rotation

Job rotation serves various functions. For those employees on the management career path, it means continuous on-the-job training. By being moved from one job to another several times in one section and then from one section to another and from one division to another, these employees learn a great deal firsthand about the company's operations.

The almost certain job rotation coming within three or four years makes all management-bound employees give top priority to their company's overall interest rather than the parochial interest of their currently assigned section or division. If a section or division wishes to raise its annual performance record at the expense of another, Hiroki and his colleagues are not likely to join in. Hiroki knows that the section chief or division manager of the group against which his own group is competing may well become his boss after the next rotation.

Job rotation also has an advantage of cutting across the maze of bureaucracy in larger companies. In every division or section, there are people who have had experience in other divisions or sections. They know the internal thinking of these groups. When coordination between them must be effected, Japanese employees can move much faster than their American counterparts. They can perform the task with less red tape, less internal conflict, less paperwork and fewer layers of authorizations to clear. Hiroki, for example, may simply go to his former division manager and colleagues to convey the thinking of his new division, serving as a liaison between the two.

Job rotation is important in preparing employees to become future top- and middle-level managers. Nemoto Masao, president of Toyoda Gosei, makes a practice of sending his best employee for rotation to another section or division. The person chosen is like an honor graduate. He has studied under his mentor, in this instance the current section chief or division manager, and learned the subject thoroughly. He goes to another division because there is nothing left to learn in his present position. Losing him may mean temporary inefficiency for the division he leaves behind because he has been such a splendid worker, but the sacrifice is worth taking for the greater good of the company. It also challenges the division to train other employees sent there in the next rotation to become as well qualified as the one they just "graduated." When properly handled, job rotation creates a collegiate atmosphere in companies.

For future managers in mid-career, job rotation provides opportunities for the company to observe their suitability for higher positions. A finance man who is a wizard with numbers, who knows the tax laws of Japan and the United States well, and who is quite at home in the accounting division, may still be passed over for promotion to division manager if in prior job rotations he is known to have neglected the manufacturing division. David Halberstam relates in great detail the role Robert McNamara played at Ford and how his cost-cutting perpetuated the run-down conditions of its plants.[1] In a Japanese company practicing job rotation, McNamara's chance of becoming president would be practically nonexistent.

The system of job rotation creates a bias towards a generalist orientation. One can be an engineer or a liberal arts graduate when entering the company. One can excel in a special area. Beyond that, however, one must become knowledgeable in different areas of the company's operations. To reach the rank of company director, one must be a dedicated person, driven to know everything about the company.

RECRUITMENT AND LONG-TERM COMMITMENT

Job rotation is an expensive proposition. No one can step into a new position and become productive immediately. In spite of this, Japanese companies are willing to practice frequent job rotations because of their belief in nurturing human resources (*jinzai*).

Many managers and regular employees experience job rotation, but only a handful emerge as company directors. If cost was viewed strictly in these terms, the expense would be prohibitive. However, the rationale in Japan is that spending a substantial sum to educate those who will not become company directors still leaves a cadre of committed middle-level executives who know all about the company. They can then set good examples for other employees to follow.

There is something very Confucian about this approach. It was the Chinese philosopher Mencius (372-289 B.C.) who spoke of governing people by setting good examples. "As the wind blows, trees and grasses will bend in the same direction," said Mencius. "So will a community when a man of virtue sets examples," he continued. That teaching became one of the key concepts in the Confucian tradition.

Mencius believed in the perfectibility of man through education. Not confined to what may be obtained from degree-granting institutions, education is experienced in day-to-day life. A company can set itself up as an educational institution to lead its employees to a higher level of attainment in the sense that Mencius and Plato would have used it. Many companies take this role seriously. One of the favorite mottoes of Matsushita is: "Matsushita Electric Company is a place to nurture people. Incidentally, it also makes electric appliances." There is a total commitment to education. Continuous education and training of employees come naturally as manifestations of this commitment.

Of course, companies do not survive by idealism alone. Educating employees is a good investment in Japan because of its exceptionally low rate of labor turnover. There is a system of so-called lifetime employment, which guarantees employment through the ages of fifty-five or sixty, but this is practiced only in larger companies. Employees of their subcontractors do not enjoy the same privilege. Estimates vary as to the number of employees covered under lifetime employment. The rate is probably lower than 40 percent and is closer to 35 percent. Lifetime employment as a concept, however, is well accepted. Even in those companies that do not adhere to it, a long-term commitment to employment is practiced both by the employers and employees. In this book the term "long-term commitment" will be frequently used, which is closer to what companies in Japan actually practice.

If a long-term commitment to employees is practiced, then recruitment should become one of the most important corporate activities, which is indeed the case. For workers, seeking a job is taken very seriously. In some instances, marrying is done more casually than seeking a career position, with both representing one's lifetime commitment. After all, the time spent with a mate is often less than that spent with colleagues in the company, and one's family cannot survive without the security afforded by the company.

Recruitment

The practice of hiring graduates fresh out of college goes back to prewar years. At that time college graduates were still a rarity and major companies wanted to have an uninterrupted supply of managerial talent. In the high-growth years of the late 1950s, recruitment geared to the academic year was extended to high school graduates to insure a supply of blue-collar workers.

Japan's academic year begins in April and ends in March. Recruitment on college campuses begins in October after the summer vacation and continues throughout the remainder of the academic year. In a company's direct recruitment, college professors play dominant roles. Company X may ask Professor Y to recommend so many students with special qualifications in certain fields. In a way it can be considered an old-boy network and connections play a key role. When this old-boy network does not provide enough candidates, a general advertisement and other direct approaches may be undertaken. The latter practice may resemble that of the United States.

Blue-collar workers are recruited from graduates of senior and junior high schools. The latter is now rare, as most young men and women prefer to continue their education at least through senior high school. Normally recruitment is done locally. For example, Toyota may recruit heavily from the Mikawa-Aichi area. When this practice does not yield enough people, recruitment may be extended nationwide, especially in the labor surplus regions of Hokkaido, Tohoku and Kyushu. When these new recruits come to work, they are placed in company dormitories, which incidentally provide an additional opportunity for employee education.

Whether the new recruit is a management-bound, salaried worker or a high school graduate wage earner, he needs a guarantor to become accepted in the company. In the case of the former, the guarantor may be his professor or some management person in the company. The latter may be his home town mayor or chamber of commerce director. These guarantors are personally known to the company and, if the new recruit violates the rules of the company, the guarantor will be asked to admonish him. In earlier days, the system of guarantor provided a bridge of communication between rural and urban Japan. Today the distinction has become somewhat blurred, but the system still serves to remind all the individuals affected of their societal obligations both to the company and to the town from which they came.

To be selected for a major company's management program requires a diploma from a reputable university. Seldom is attention paid to the academic records, however. The method of selection varies from company to company, but usually includes an intensive personal interview or interviews. The personality of the prospective employee is carefully assessed. If he is a loner, unable to get along well with others, his chance for employment is greatly diminished. Altogether, the system is geared toward securing good team players for the company.

A written examination may also be given and this is the form favored by most major newspapers. Mainichi, Japan's third largest daily, for example, gives a multiple choice examination to test candidates' liberal arts background, general knowledge and writing skills. In its organization, the test resembles that of the U.S. Foreign Service examination.[2]

Dentsu, the advertising conglomerate, asks its employees to fulfill two separate functions. The first is to remain creative. The second is to be able to work in the world arena, shoulder to shoulder with diplomats and industrial moguls. These two functions can be mutually exclusive. Copywriters must be allowed their intellectual freedom and unconventionality. As Dentsu department heads state, "We don't mind our copywriters working stark naked if they can produce good ad copies." While such behavior is not known to exist, the copywriters as a group are unconventional in their appearance, and they are allowed to remain so in their Tsukiji headquarters only a few blocks from Ginza. At the same time, the international marketing group people can look and act like diplomats par excellence with their pin-striped blue suits. Incidentally, they are the ones who successfully cornered the advertising market for their clients in the 1984 Los Angeles Olympics.

The two groups are so different one might think that in their recruitment two totally separate approaches had been applied. But that was not the case. There was another overriding consideration: the company must remain one, and there must be a uniform system of recruitment to insure that it remains a solid team.

Dentsu is a glamorous company to work for and receives many applicants. A large number are referred by politically and industrially well-connected people. In addition, there is a large group of new graduates who appear at its door to be interviewed. Dentsu's answer has been a simple, yet effective one. Like newspaper companies, it gives a written entrance examination but not much emphasis is placed on it. As one supervisor remarks, "There are so many good examination scores that you cannot base your judgment on them." Instead, it relies heavily on three tiers of interviews. The first interview is done by young people from groups interested in hiring new employees. This is followed by another interview conducted by young people not related to the hiring group in the company. The two interviews are intended to make the applicants feel at ease while talking freely with their "peers." By having two groups examine the same candidates, the company attempts to weed out those who can be too easily typecast into a certain category. The successful candidates are then interviewed by top management. Top management is committed to spending as many days as needed to complete the interviews requested by middle management and the hiring groups, especially the copywriting and other creative departments. The politically well connected may not survive the first round while an odd but creative person may be eliminated at the final top-level interview. The result is a fine mix of creative people in pin-striped blue or grey flannel suits set to enter the employ of Dentsu. The ability to act as a team is thus preserved.

The most unusual recruitment practices are reported by Nihon Densan, which supplies ultra-small motors for personal computers, video cassette players, medical optical instruments and jet airplanes. Started in 1973, it now has a little over 700 employees. One year its president, Nagamori Shigenobu, ordered all the candidates assembled to eat breakfast, and timed them. He then hired those who finished within ten minutes. In another year, he chose new employees exclusively from those who were rejected for jobs the previous year. In yet another year, he asked the candidates to clean toilet bowls barehanded and personally inspected the results. Some left in disgust, but enough people remained to complete the assignment and were hired. Nagamori, of course, has his detractors, but the reasoning behind his actions is worthy of note. If a person is willing to keep his surroundings clean, he will keep the bathrooms, including the toilet bowls, spic-and-span at all times. Cleaning bathrooms is one chore he imposes on all of his employees. It sends a clear-cut message that the workplace must be kept clean. In an electronics business that supplies precision mini-motors and computer parts, cleanliness is imperative. It is the first step toward quality control and toward effective teamwork.[3]

Educating New Employees

The arrival of new employees infuses new blood into the mainstream of company management and becomes an important occasion for the company. The president may greet everyone individually and send letters to the families of new employees conveying his personal appreciation. Their education may begin in Zen temples or company auditoriums and dormitories. Wherever held, it conveys the message of a common destiny. "We are in this together," a company president may say, using the Japanese phrase *ichiren takusho*. The phrase originally comes from Buddhism, which speaks of going together to paradise and residing on the same petal of the lotus. From that it has taken on the meaning of "for better or worse people must work together and share the same fate." This notion of sharing the same destiny is drilled constantly into the minds of new workers.

Just as new draftees to a sports team can make a difference between winning or losing, new employees in a company can provide impetus for creating a new winning combination. "Management officers, knowing the company's ordinary business is being done by energetic and enthusiastic younger employees, can devote their time and effort to planning the future of the company," says Morita Akio of Sony. "In the long run, your business and its future are in the hands of the people you hire," he continues. "To put it a bit more dramatically, the fate of your business is actually in the hands of the youngest recruit on the staff."[4]

Morita is not alone in this assessment. Each class of new recruits is carefully observed not only by the company that hired them but also by other companies. *The Japan Company Handbook*, published semiannually in English and quarterly in Japanese by Toyo Keizai, cites the average age of company employees in each of the entries for Japanese companies whose stocks are traded in various exchanges. The prestigious Nikkei Business, research arm of the *Nihon Keizai Shimbun* (*Japan*

Economic Journal), uses the average age as one of the criteria in judging a company's performance.[5] Nikkei Business reasons that the higher the average age the smaller the number of recent recruits, which shows an inherent weakness in the company.

On-the-job training is intensive, taking the form of apprenticeship at times. Young employees' opinions are sought, however, and they are allowed to make mistakes. Mistakes are considered part of the learning process; avoiding recurrences is what matters. In any event, mentors around the trainees can subtly correct the mistakes without embarrassing them. Training does not follow precise training manuals or memos from superiors. The way things are done is transmitted by the example set by superiors and colleagues, and by the instructions given to them orally. Early in their training, the employees may be given a small project or two to complete. They may be told to go ahead without receiving written instructions. They are encouraged to take initiatives and, when in doubt, get into the habit of asking. In a sense, the superiors are delegating power to these new employees and teaching them how to handle it responsively. The entire process is geared toward making young employees feel they belong there as members of the team.

One of the best uses of on-the-job training is demonstrated by Fujitsu, the computer manufacturer. It recruits engineering graduates from top universities and immediately places them in the design division to design large mainframe computers. After two or three years in the design division, these young engineers are transferred to the manufacturing division to produce the computers they themselves designed. Then after three or more years in manufacturing, these engineers are sent out as systems engineers or engaged in technical sales to operate, service and sell the computers they designed and manufactured.

This system gives the company several advantages. After five years, most engineers reach the point of burnout and require new training. It is at this juncture that they are sent to become closer to customers. They can be the best technical sales people and systems engineers because they know the computers inside out. When there are complaints from the customers, they can take note and immediately transmit them to the new crop of design engineers, who are their *kohai* or junior in rank. What they say carries a lot of weight, unlike the complaints American salesmen transmit to their home offices. Their closeness to the customers helps the design engineers do a better job of creating new computers. Everyone can take pride in what the company produces as a team.

THE ART OF CONSENSUS BUILDING

Japanese words like *ringi* and *nemawashi* refer to the process of consensus building. *Ringi* refers to the process of circulating a proposal for approval among the affected parties in the office. When one person finishes reading the *ringi* document, he affixes his seal (vermilion chop) and sends it off to the next person on the list. The document can be very impressive looking when it completes its round covered with many vermilion chops.

In its function, the *ringi* document resembles that of an interoffice memo in the United States that affected parties initial or check off their names. Unlike these memos, however, which can be issued indiscriminately, *ringi* has a clearly assigned place in Japanese office procedure. It is utilized when a proposal is not important enough to be placed before a formal conference but significant enough to be put in writing, because it cannot be delegated to informal discussions.

Nemawashi is a term used in gardening. If a large tree is to be transplanted, the gardener must make up his mind a year or two before it is to take place. He must dig a trench about three feet deep and eighteen inches wide around the tree, about five feet from the trunk. All roots that pass through the trench must be cut, leaving thin or fibrous roots to produce new young feeding roots. Figuratively, the term is now used in business to suggest that long before a project is undertaken all affected parties must be consulted. We speak of "touching base" with concerned parties in this country, but *nemawashi* goes a step further. It also implies that opposition to the project under consideration must be nipped in the bud and support for it carefully cultivated.

The practice of *ringi* and *nemawashi* has enabled middle management in Japan to build consensus and minimize internal conflict. For example, they may agree to undertake a certain project and iron out their differences ahead of time. This practice has also facilitated better project implementations.

Ringi and *nemawashi* do not imply, however, that decision-making power is widely shared. There are two constraining factors. One is the hierarchical nature of Japanese society. In the words of the Tokyo University anthropologist Nakae Chie, Japan is a vertical society. In decision making, vertical ties are crucial, and consensus building among peers in the horizontal direction has to yield to vertical authority. There are certain matters that do not render themselves to consensus building. Decisions regarding personnel, for example, require delicate handling, even secrecy.

WHO MAKES DECISIONS?

The decision-making process is not drastically different between American corporations and Japanese companies when narrowed to the issue of how many people are involved in making key decisions. What *is* different are the perceptions of those affected by a particular decision. Workers in Japan often feel they have had a part in the process, whereas in the United States that sense of participation normally does not exist.

To the question of how decisions are reached in their respective companies, this writer received the following answers:

Line workers, average age thirty-two:

We have our own QC (quality control) circle, which meets every other week. We usually choose a topic on something which troubles us and requires improvement. There are things we can do on our own, but there are others for which we must have the help of our supervisor. But we are quite happy with what we are doing.

Members of a section, average age twenty-six:

If we find a problem, the eight of us go around to get all the information we need. We consult with people in other sections and we talk to our section chief. If the chief says yes, we go ahead with our own solutions. Yes, we make some decisions on our own.

A division manager, age forty-six:

The function of a division manager is to transmit to his subordinates what the top thinks and to transmit to the top what the subordinates recommend. I am standing at the crossroad to facilitate the smooth flow of traffic. Well, I help our president make some decisions on matters relating to my division but he is the one who really makes them.

The significance of these responses is that almost everyone in the company feels he has some input in decision making. It is also significant, however, that everyone, including the division manager, defers to his superior. One possible inference is that decisions are made at the highest level. When it is known, however, that the lower-level managers adhere faithfully to the company's general guidelines, the power of decision making may be delegated to them.

Presidency of a Company — Dentsu's Tamaru

Decisions regarding personnel matters at the highest level are often made by one person alone. Tamaru Hideharu tells a poignant story of how he was chosen as Dentsu's seventh president.

One day in the late spring of 1977, Tamaru, then a senior executive director of Dentsu, received an urgent summons from President Nakahata's office. As he approached Nakahata's office, he thought to himself, "I am sixty-three now. If the president wants me to retire, I shall say I am ready." He had risen through the ranks since his entry into Dentsu at the age of thirty-four in 1948. Prior to that he was a history teacher in an obscure middle school. He had not been one of those Dentsu men who took pride in being nurtured by the system since their graduation. He looked back on his own record since the day of his transfer to the executive office in 1965; it had been good, but not spectacular by Dentsu's standards. He was ready to accept the worst.

Nakahata cordially greeted him. Then came the surprise: "I plan to retire, and I am naming you as my successor." Speechless, all Tamaru could think was that he wanted a couple of weeks to think it over. Suddenly he realized that a great burden had descended on his shoulders.

As Nakahata had expected, Tamaru proved to be a worthy successor, making Dentsu into a "global communications company" whose annual sales would reach one trillion yen under his reign. "There was nothing in my background — my love of poetry, my major in Japanese history — that would have endeared me to a committee selecting a Dentsu president," said Tamaru. "I pride myself in being a good teacher, guiding those who are younger than I in fulfilling their dreams. But that would not be enough. Mr. Nakahata knew, however, that I shared the vision he had for Dentsu. And perhaps that was all that mattered. When you become president, your own perception changes dramatically. You want to name someone who can continue your work. In a way, I became a cog in the continuity called Dentsu."[6]

Corporate Merger — Toyota Motors

Personnel is not the only affair that must be exempt from the consensus-building process. An equally persuasive case can be made for matters relating to corporate merger.

On July 1, 1982, Toyota Automobile Manufacturing and Toyota Motor Sales officially merged, ending thirty-two years of separate existence to form the present Toyota Motors Corporation.

Toyoda Eiji, a first cousin of the founder of the company, was the man behind this decision. Eiji became president of Toyota Automobile Manufacturing in 1967. Since 1969, he had been thinking of merging the two entities. The sales and manufacturing companies did not always see eye to eye, and the public often saw them as two companies bickering continuously among themselves. Anomaly also existed overseas where dealers first contacted by the manufacturing company had to sign contracts with the sales company. To Eiji, the question of corporate identity was a paramount one. The two entities were one company until they were forced to separate in 1950. By 1982, there were not many employees who could remember that the two entities had been one. The longer he waited the less chance there was of the two merging smoothly.

Eiji consulted one person, Kamiya Shotaro, the Toyota Sales president. When Kamiya showed no enthusiasm, however, Eiji did not pursue the matter further. The merger did not take place until after Kamiya's death. Then, only four persons were consulted by Eiji before an accord for merger was reached in December 1981. They were Toyoda Shoichiro, son of the founder, who was then president of Toyota Sales; Kato Masayuki, chairman of Toyota Sales; Hanai Shohachi, chairman of Toyota Automobile Manufacturing; and Okamoto Tojiro, a senior member of the Toyota establishment. Secrecy was maintained throughout in reaching this merger accord creating Japan's largest corporation.[7]

In addition to personnel and merger, matters relating to structural changes, increasing the company's capitalization and purchase of real estate are normally handled with the least amount of employee participation. Consensus building must be set aside in favor of maintaining secrecy.

With many areas of corporate decision exclusively in the hands of top management, the decision-making process may resemble that of the United States. There are still two vital differences, however. First, in Japanese companies a perception persists that others do share in the decision-making process;

second, decisions are made more quickly without the intervention of various committees.

Once a decision is made, a Japanese company can implement it quickly. The layers of responsibility or authority separating top management from line workers are far fewer in Japan than in the United States. The company's ability for implementation is further strengthened by top management's willingness to delegate power to middle management, the sections and the workplace. Quality circles are utilized effectively as a means of communicating to all workers the decision reached or goals set and the method of implementation.

REFLECTIONS

The Japanese practices of lifetime employment, job rotation and sharing of responsibilities have created a system of management that is relatively fumble free in international competition. The following advantages are enjoyed by the Japanese:

1. Retention of key personnel via a predictable career path for each

2. Teamwork with relative absence of internal conflict

3. Ability to identify with the overall interest of the company

4. Reduction in paperwork

Adopting the Japanese system in its totality in the United States is obviously not possible, but some of its outstanding features can be applied by American companies with benefit. In this section, a summary of each advantage is followed by a short checklist to be used by American managers in comparing notes with Japanese practices.

1. Retention of Key Personnel through Career Pathing

When a new project is to be initiated, or a new position filled, an American company may suddenly find there is no one who can fill it. Talent grown in the company has been lured away by a competitor, and at this critical juncture, the company must go outside to find someone to head this new project. A search committee is quickly organized which goes through a series of interviews and finally settles on a candidate from a competitor at a considerable expense to the company. This does not happen in a Japanese company.

Through lifetime employment, career pathing, job rotation and continuous training, the Japanese company can quickly assign a person to handle the new project. In fact, there are others waiting in the wings, ready to be assigned to projects that may not materialize until two or three years later. Japanese managers can look to the future confidently in planning the company's strategies.

Without the lifetime employment system, an American company can still create a system that will secure long-term commitment from its employees, obtain their loyalty and enjoy the advantages that Japanese companies possess. Now let us turn to our checklist:

Does my company provide job security? When there is a recession, my first reaction is to:
  · Lay off workers.
  · Cut pay across the board, shorten the work week and engage in other burden-sharing activities to ensure retaining the services of the employees.

Do we promote from within?

Do we have an adequate system of investing in the professional and personal growth of our employees?

2. Teamwork with Relative Absence of Internal Conflict

Each individual has a way of doing things that is right for him. One person's right way, however, may be wrong for another; when these people work together conflict becomes inevitable.

One of the basic aims of an organization is to reduce these conflicts and channel individuals' energies toward cooperative and more productive ends. In American companies, unfortunately, practices tend to accentuate and not diminish conflicts between individuals. We see individuals in our companies who want to make themselves look good and deny credit to others. We see some refusing to extend a helping hand to others in the same office because it may make their own records look less outstanding by comparison. We see meaningless contests for trips to Hawaii or Florida, salesmen undercutting their fellow salesmen without creating a single extra sale for the company. All of these ills have been created in the name of providing incentives. American managers must recognize, however, that no matter how good the quarterback's arm, without his teammates, he may end up compiling the record for quarterback sacks instead of receiving his Super Bowl ring. No one can be an island unto himself in the corporate world.

The Japanese practices of *ringi*, *nemawashi*, and slow promotion enhance teamwork and reduce internal conflict. When a project is successfully completed, it is the team that receives the praise. Individuals are not singled out for recognition, no matter how great their contributions may be. Likewise, rewards are given to the group and not to individuals. There may not be an expense-paid trip for the employee and his spouse to Hawaii, but the company may pay for a weekend trip to Atami, the hot spring spa, for the entire group.

When a project fails, conversely it is not the individuals but the entire group that shares the blame. Under such circumstances, there is no need for finger pointing and blaming others for the mistakes made. Truth can come out quickly, which in turn can assist the group in undertaking steps to prevent recurrence.

Japanese companies can compete effectively because they have learned how to work as a team. Mori Motonari (1497-1571), a warlord in Western Japan, assembled his three children at his deathbed and gave each an arrow to break. The arrows were broken easily. He then asked that three arrows be bound together. The three children took turns trying to break the bound arrows but without success. Individually, the arrows offered no resistance, but together they were formidable. That lesson was not forgotten by the Mori heirs and certainly not by the rest of the country in the generations to come.

"By uniting we stand, by dividing we fall," is a line from the liberty song of 1768. Teamwork has also been a tradition in the United States. We can work as a team if we choose to do so, and here is our checklist:

When I give assignments, do I make them into educational experiences for my staff members?
- Can the assignment be given to a team and not to individuals?
- Is there any provision in the assignment that would require different types of expertise to complete, forcing team members to learn from each other?

Can the ladder of promotion in title be slowed down for the incoming class of new employees?
- Does my company reward teamwork?
- Do we promote team players?
- Do we promote ego-centered stars?

Do we have excessive individual merit categories in salary determination?
- Do we base our bonuses on individual performance?
- On team performance?
- Both?

When two of my key staff members are at odds with each other, my reactions are: (check as many items as applicable)
- Tell them to shut up and not do their fighting on company time.
- Tell them to resolve their differences within the next forty-eight hours.
- Meet with them individually.
- Call a meeting to resolve their differences.
- Have one of them transferred out of my division.
- Have.both of them transferred.

In Japan infighting is never encouraged, and when two members disagree, they are asked to resolve their disputes on their own without referring them to a higher authority. The disdain for public conflict is so strong that both parties are often punished, even though one party is judged to be right. Regulations for the residents of Edo issued in 1655 contains the following provision: "Article 1. Parties engaged in public brawls and quarrels are punishable by death according to the law, irrespective of whichever party is in the right or at fault." Of course, there is no similar criminal code in modern-day Japan, but the tradition of punishing both parties still survives, creating an effective deterrent to conflict.

3. Identification with the Overall Interest of the Company

Job rotation in Japan has created a group of dedicated managers who identify with the overall interest of their company and not with the parochial interest of certain sections or divisions. They are eager to know everything about their own company and can serve as effective channels of communication between different divisions of the company.

Their frequent comings and goings between different divisions also allow them to transfer new technology and information from one division to another. Teamwork existing in sections and divisions is spread to the entire company through job rotation. Now here is our checklist:

Does my company have an effective system of human resources development through job rotation?

As a manager, am I willing to allow my best staff member to be transferred to another division through job rotation?
- Do I consider job rotation a means of getting rid of undesirable staff members?
- Do I consider it an opportunity to train future managers for the company?

When there is a matter that requires participation by other divisions to resolve, am I willing to delegate authority to my staff members to engage in negotiation?
- Am I willing to let them make mistakes?
- Do I still take responsibility for what they have done?

4. Reduction in Paperwork

One of the by-products of lifetime employment, slow promotion and job rotation is that employees get to know each other. When these employees work together in offices "without walls," their deliberations become less formal. Where memos in triplicate may be required in American companies, an oral presentation will suffice in Japan. The paperwork load is much lighter, and there is less bureaucracy to contend with. In this way, Japanese companies become better equipped to take bold and timely action when called for than their American counterparts.

In smaller companies, this procedure is even simpler. Honda Electronics specializes in producing transistorized color sonar fish-school detectors, sonar search lights, body scanners, ultrasound wave microscopes and other instruments on the cutting edge of high technology. Established in 1956 in Toyohashi, to the east of Nagoya, it now has 140 employees. The technology control section is directly under the supervision of its president,

Honda Keisuke. All twelve of its other sections and offices are combined into four teams of design, manufacturing, sales and administration that again report directly to the president.

Employees gather freely and informally to discuss issues among themselves or with their team leader, who in appearance and action is "one of the boys" and indistinguishable from the rest. Decisions are made quickly and sometimes orally on the spot by the president. The company has not had any unresolved issues that caused later difficulties. Appropriately there is a slogan pasted on the wall that reads: "SIMPLE IS BEST." Now is the time to turn to our checklist:

Do we really need this memo?
  · Does it help someone do a better job?
  · Can we agree on the contents with a phone call or a face-to-face discussion?
  · Am I writing this memo simply to protect myself?
  · Am I creating additional and unnecessary work for the ones who receive this memo, and for my secretary?

Do I encourage excessive memo writing by my staff members?
  · Do I insist on their supplying supporting documents I have no intention of reading?
  · Do I fail to respond to their important requests so that they are forced to write second and third memos?

Am I accessible to my staff members?
  · Can they drop in on me freely?
  · If not, do I have an informal hour when they can come in to chat with me without going through my secretaries?
  · Do I occasionally go to the person's desk instead of asking him to come to see me?

How often do I ask this question of myself and of my staff members: "How can we simplify our structure?"
  · Am I addicted to the organizational chart?
  · Do I always insist on going through channels?

It is always important to remember that good management begins with good personnel management. Long before the West started using the term "human resources," the Japanese had the term *jinzai*. They knew that the first step toward creating a winning team was to show appreciation for team members by fostering its human resources.

CHAPTER 3

Enduring Corporate Culture

A company is a living organization that transmits its values from one generation to another. It also has a distinctive way of doing things. An IBM employee has a special way of dressing or speaking and somehow differentiates himself from an employee of Hewlett-Packard. A GM man talks differently from a Chrysler man. There is a thing called corporate culture, and in Japan it is known as *shafu*. Literally, the term means the way the wind blows in a company, or the fashion of the company. Kenkyusha's *New Japanese-English Dictionary* translates the term as "the ways of a company; a company's custom [tradition]."

A winning tradition is a precious thing that must be kept within the "family," which is the company. A time of joint suffering should be remembered because it creates a stronger bond to bind the family members. Companies thrive on their own legends to foster these shared values. More often than not, however, they rely on their corporate philosophies as a means of transmitting their values.

CORPORATE PHILOSOPHY

A corporate philosophy is normally a simple document con-

taining the founder's ideals, moral injunctions, and later addi-
tions and amendments. Japan's oldest known corporate
philosophy is the "House Laws of the Mitsui Family," which
goes back over three centuries.

Mitsubishi in Early Days

Mitsui's modern rival, Mitsubishi, was established as a ship-
ping company after purchasing from the government surplus
ships used in the Taiwan expedition of 1874. In 1876, this fledgling
company was in the throes of a fierce battle for control of
Japan's coastal trade against the well established British Penin-
sula & Oriental Steam Navigation Company. On that occasion, Iwasaki Yataro, the company's founder, wrote to his employees:

> I now propose to do my utmost, and along with my 35 million compa-
> triots, to perform my duty as a citizen of this country. That is to re-
> cover the right of coastal trade in our hands, and not to delegate that
> task to foreigners.... There have been many who wish to hinder our
> progress in fulfilling our obligations.... The Peninsula & Oriental
> Steam Navigation Company comes to compete for the right of coastal
> navigation with us by setting up a new line between Yokohama and
> Shanghai, and is attempting to claim its right over the ports of
> Nagasaki, Kobe and Yokohama.... Our company is young and not
> every phase of its operation is well conducted. In contrast, the P & O
> Company is backed by its massive capital, its large fleet of ships and by
> its experiences of operations in Oriental countries. In competing
> against this giant, what methods can we employ?
>   I have thought about this problem very carefully and have come to
> one conclusion. There is no other alternative but to eliminate un-
> necessary positions and unnecessary expenditures. This is a time-worn
> solution and no new wisdom is involved.... Starting immediately I
> propose that we engage in this task. By eliminating unnecessary per-
> sonnel from the payroll, eliminating unnecessary expenditures and
> engaging in hard and arduous work, we shall be able to solidify the
> foundation of our company. If there is a will there is a way. Through
> our own effort, we shall be able to repay the government for its protec-
> tion and answer our nation for its confidence shown in us. Let us work
> together in discharging our responsibilities and not be ashamed of our-

selves. Whether we succeed or fail, whether we can gain profit or sustain loss, we cannot anticipate at this time.... If we succeed it will not only be an accomplishment for our company alone but also a glorious event for our Japanese Empire, which shall let its light shine to all four corners of the earth. We can succeed or fail, and it depends on your effort or lack of it. Do your utmost in this endeavor![2]

Two years later, Iwasaki incorporated these exhortations in a more formal document, indicating how he wanted his company to be managed. His letter and the 1878 document were precursors of today's corporate philosophy. The lean and mean management style and international competitiveness by which Mitsubishi is known today are foreshadowed in these documents.

Dentsu — The Advertising Giant

Corporate philosophies are modified from time to time to reflect the current state of affairs. Yoshida Hideo became president of Dentsu in 1947, two years after the end of World War II. In 1951 when the Japanese economy showed signs of recovery, giving promise to advertising activities, Yoshida exhorted Dentsu employees to ever greater efforts in his now famous "Ten Spartan Rules."[3]

1. Create work for yourself; don't wait for it to be assigned to you.

2. Take the initiative in performing your job instead of playing a passive part.

3. Grapple with big jobs — petty tasks debase you.

4. Choose difficult jobs. Progress lies in accomplishing difficult work.

5. Once you start a task, never give up — complete it, no matter what.

6. Lead those around you. Leading others instead of being led makes a big difference in the long run.

7. Have a plan. A long-term plan engenders perseverance, planning and effort, and gives you hope for the future.

8. Have self-confidence. Otherwise, your work will lack force, persistence and even substance.

9. Use your brain to the fullest degree at all times. Keep an eye on all quarters and always be on the alert. This is the way we ensure satisfactory service.

10. Don't be afraid of friction. Friction is the mother of progress and the stimulus for aggressiveness. If you fear friction, you will become servile and timid.

The "ten rules" now constitute the base of Dentsu's corporate philosophy, but a tradition has also developed that permits Yoshida's successors to supplement these rules from time to time. Such was the case when Tamaru Hideharu gave his New Year's message in 1979, looking forward to the coming of the twenty-first century. Tamaru's points were contained in five principles:

1. Go one step further

2. Broaden your sphere

3. Listen carefully to what others have to say

4. Have your own viewpoint, and

5. Don't forget the spirit of the founder and the tenacity of our predecessors.

Tamaru's five principles were an attempt to find a common meeting ground for teamwork and creativity. He explains his third principle in the following words:

An individual's capability is limited. In contrast, the creative power that springs from solidarity is immeasurable. In teamwork, it is indispensable to listen carefully to what others say. By listening to others, you can eliminate discontinuity, remove prejudices and avoid dogmatism. The first step in producing excellent work is to give careful consideration to the feelings and opinions of others. Broadening your sphere is the seed of creativity.

In a continuously changing modern world, an advertising company requires a creative tension; hence Tamaru's fourth principle, "Have your own viewpoint." As Tamaru says, "The company needs all kinds of people of all kinds who possess a strong sense of individuality. Dentsu should be the organic integration of such people. When Dentsu is organized in that way, it will be able to see things from many different angles, respond to all kinds of situations, of all kinds, and make a bold leap toward total creativity." That summarizes well the corporate culture of Dentsu.

YKK — The Zipper King

Yoshida Tadao (b. 1908) is the head of YKK, which has forty manufacturing plants of zippers and aluminum doors and 140 offices around the world. It now controls as much as three-fourths of the world market share in zippers. From a humble beginning in 1934, when he started his company with only two employees, Yoshida can now claim to have friends among the famous and powerful, including a president of the United States — Jimmy Carter.

As a youth, Yoshida was fascinated by the life of Andrew Carnegie. He was especially impressed by Carnegie's words, "Surplus wealth is a sacred trust which its possessor is bound to administer in his lifetime for the good of the community." His corporate philosophy is a direct takeoff from Carnegie's dictum: "Sow the seeds of goodness and do good, then goodness is bound to be rewarded. Do not take but give. By giving, more is given back to the giver. There is in this world a thing called endless recycling of goodness."[4]

Yoshida applies his philosophy of "endless recycling of goodness" in managing his company and in labor negotiations. For example, at one time repatriation of profits from its overseas companies was a big issue at YKK. Yoshida's answer was simple. "We cannot remove profits from the host countries. We can accept the interest payments on our investment and nothing more. A bridge once built must not be withdrawn" if the principle of "endless recycling of goodness" is to be fully applied.

Another time, the 8,000 employees at YKK's main plant in Kurobe wanted to form an employee cooperative. It was a good idea because with 8,000 members participating, they had a large combined purchasing power. Yoshida opposed this move strenuously, however. The town's people had been good to the plant; if an employee cooperative were to be established, many store owners would be greatly affected. This was against the basic principle of "recycling of goodness," through which the plant would return kindness to the town.

A corporate philosophy is not a manual for employees and need not give directions for day-to-day operation of the company. It articulates the goals of the company and can be used as a means of education and exhortation. Moreover, by giving superordinate aspirations, it can help employees identify values that apply beyond the confines of the company.

A corporate philosophy can also be utilized to simplify paperwork. When there is a definite consensus about the goals, they need not be elaborated further. Or, when there is doubt about which way a decision should be made, referring to the corporate philosophy may give a clear-cut direction. YKK often chooses a plant site in less convenient rural areas, even though it may be costlier to the company. The guiding principle, however, is the "endless recycling of goodness." The site chosen is one where the plant can do the greatest good, not where it can maximize profits. At Takara Belmont, whether to enter a specific foreign market may be decided by referring to its corporate philosophy, "The World Is One," and then the company's bias is clear. When employees are inculcated with these same values, delegating power to them becomes much easier. As for matters of mundane day-to-day operation, annual policy control measures may be adopted as Nemoto Masao has done at Toyoda Gosei. This issue will be discussed in the chapter on quality control.

TRANSMITTING CORPORATE VALUES

A written corporate philosophy is one of the most effective means of transmitting corporate values. There are, however, other equally effective, nonverbal forms of transmission: through commonly held ceremonies or through the examples set by corporate executives.

Seibu — Real Estate, Hotel Chains and Railways

A most unusual practice of transmitting corporate values from one generation to another is found at Seibu, a conglomerate owning department stores, real estate, hotel chains and railways.

On the gentle hills overlooking the historic city of Kamakura by the Pacific, thirty miles to the west of Tokyo, is a massive memorial park. On one of its choicest lots is the grave of Tsutsumi Yasujiro, the founder of the Seibu group. On April 16, 1965, the first anniversary of Tsutsumi's death, a few of his loyal former employees assembled at the grave site and began the tradition of an overnight "grave watch." Two or three employees come to Kamakura after work, usually beginning at 5:00 in the evening, and remain until 8:30 the next morning. They sweep the grave site and, at 6:00 P.M. and 8:00 A.M., ring the temple bell in memory of the founder. The night is spent at a spartan rest house by the grave. This practice has continued uninterrupted every night for more than two decades since 1965.

It is a moving story, very Japanese in its poignancy. In the olden days when the feudal lord died, some of his most beloved samurai followed him in death. When this custom was banned in 1682 by the Bakufu (Shogunate), by decree, some of the samurai denounced the world and remained at the side of the departed master's grave until death also claimed their lives. The Seibu grave watch does not have these trappings of the feudal past, however. At first it was merely a suggestion by some of the old-timers that "the boss might feel kind of lonely there, all alone." It became a tradition, however, because it proved useful in the Seibu group's survival as a modern enterprise.

Participation in the grave watch is strictly voluntary, of course, but there are more volunteers than space can accommodate. In reality, participants are carefully chosen to include one veteran employee and one or two young employees. The latter may come from the same company, but often from different companies within the Seibu group. At Kamakura, with the exception of the sounding of the temple gong and the sweeping of the grave, there is no other chore. The long evening hours are spent talking about Seibu's management philosophy in the awesome presence of the founder's "spirit," which can still be keenly felt. Knowledge about the company is thus effectively transmitted from one generation of Seibu men to another generation of Seibu men.[5]

Corporate culture has many manifestations. It is the way of doing things that is special to that company. There is a common understanding both spoken and unspoken. A word that means one thing in one company may mean something different in another company. People in the same company, however, have only one interpretation they share in common. As employees work together for many years, their mutual understanding becomes so intense that sometimes they joke about knowing each other's habits better than their immediate family members. *That* is corporate culture.

In Seibu, this corporate identity is especially strong, inasmuch as many employees come from the same regions and from families of first generation Seibu employees. In effect, second-generation Seibu men are educated twice in the Seibu way, once at home and again at the company. The practice of grave watch reinforces these existing strong ties.

When Yasujiro died in 1964, his son and heir Yoshiaki was only twenty-nine. In the age-conscious Japanese society, he was too young to rule over the Seibu group. In those difficult days, when management decisions were to be made, they were always couched in terms of "what would our founder have done?" Yoshiaki emerged out of his father's shadow only after he turned forty. But he still insists that "my dad taught me everything I know. Dad still lives in me." As a major figure in Japanese industry, well known for his articulation of management philosophy, Yoshiaki still finds comfort in being identified with the founding days of the company.

Naigai News — A Newspaper Company

Returning to the founder's ideal is not confined to the Seibu group or to large companies. Naigai News is a weekly newspaper company, established in 1972 by Hasegawa Saiji, a prominent newsman once president of the Jiji Press, one of Japan's two major news organizations.

When Hasegawa died in 1977, the noted economist Kiuchi Nobutane and other friends formed an editorial board to assist the company. An advisor's group was also formed with Kiuchi at its head, including Inayama Yoshihiro, former president of the Keidanren; Hasegawa Shigenori, head of the Kansai association of economic organizations; and Hasegawa Takashi, former Minister of Labor and former Minister of Transport, among others.

Prominent as these people are, when a policy decision is to be made and differences cannot be resolved, the one question that Kiuchi asks is "What would Mr. Hasegawa have done if he were here today?" In this way, the continuity of the company is kept intact. Its current president Kiyomiya Ryu is a well-known journalist in his own right. He experiments with new ideas and cherishes his journalistic freedom. Yet the tradition set by Hasegawa is an invisible ally in managing the present company. *Sekai to Nippon* (The World and Japan) is a weekly journal of opinion with a large portion of its articles contributed by experts in the field. Those who once wrote for Hasegawa remain loyal to the company under Kiyomiya, helping retain previous subscribers. In the meantime, Kiyomiya reaches out to new readers. The paper is now debt free, recovering from the bad years after Hasegawa's death. Appropriately, for its fifteenth anniversary celebration in 1987, it has chosen to publish Hasegawa's essays in a commemorative volume. It is also engaged in an ongoing project of assessing mass media's role in contemporary society. This, incidentally, was a favorite subject of Hasegawa.

Paradoxical as it may seem, those companies emphasizing corporate philosophy, returning to the basics and returning to the founder's ideals, also pay greater attention to detail. The latter is almost a dividend for doing the former well. It is like a football team that knows all about running and passing games; all they have to worry about is the detailed strategy for the next encounter.

Good modern Japanese managers can identify with the following passage from *Hagakure* (Hidden behind the leaves), a basic book on the way of the samurai (or *bushido*) completed in 1716:

> Lord Nabeshima Naoshige's precepts contain an injunction saying, "On grave matters, deliberations must be light." To this Ishida Kazue adds a commentary. "On minor matters, deliberations must be heavy." There are not likely to be more than two or three grave matters occurring in one's lifetime. You can carefully deliberate on these matters every day, and understand their full meanings. Therefore think ahead of time, and when an important event takes place, recall what you have already deliberated and act accordingly. You can accomplish whatever is necessary effortlessly. On the other hand, if you do not think of these grave matters daily, and try to make a simple judgment on arriving at the scene, you will meet failure and cannot take an appropriate action....[6]

By being diligent with the basics, modern managers can deliberate carefully on minor details.

MANAGING THROUGH EXAMPLES

In creating a viable corporate culture, a good example set by the chief executive is more powerful than a thousand words of injunction.

Komaki Hot Spring Spa

Sugimoto Yukio presides over a hot spring resort hotel complex located near the city of Misawa, in the northern part of Honshu. Known as the Komaki Hot Spring Spa, there are three major hotels on this 123-acre site. The hotels combine Japanese- and Western-style accommodations and are linked together by huge, completely walled corridors. These corridors then lead to the main attraction, the hot spring spa. Bathers traveling through the corridors clad only in their *yukata* (bathrobes) are treated to various attractions including a folk art museum, a replica of a Tohoku region farm house with farm implements from a bygone era, smaller-sized replicas of some major castle rooms and a little shrine at which to wish for procreation that then leads into a wedding hall.

Outside these walled corridors is the garden — named the Festival Fish Cave Park — which Mr. Sugimoto can boast to be the largest in the world. It has a traditional tea house and a huge pond dedicated to Kappa, a legendary semiaquatic being who is supposedly endowed with human intelligence. Sugimoto's annual festival for Kappa is a major local attraction drawing thousands of visitors.

Hotel rooms are sold out most weekends and during the week the occupancy rate remains exceptionally high. This defies conventional wisdom. Misawa is merely an intermediate stop between Aomori, the northernmost major city on the island of

Honshu, and Morioka, the terminus of the Northeastern bullet train. It is close to the middle of nowhere, but tourists come in droves, partly due to Sugimoto's skillful promotion. He can sell dreams and in his deft hands Kappa becomes a Japanese equivalent of Mickey Mouse. There is another persuasive reason, however — the hotels and the grounds are kept meticulously clean at all times.

A striking part of Sugimoto's management, however, is that his maintenance cost is minimal. Workers and guests alike help keep his park and hotel complex clean. Sugimoto loves to stroll around his park and chat with his guests. A number of years ago, he saw a lot of cigarette butts and paper strewn around the park and decided to do something about it. He did not write memos, but as he strolled he used a stick or his bare hands to pick up refuse. The maids, seeing what their president was doing, imitated him. Soon, some of the guests started doing the same. Before long, no one threw anything on the ground. Setting a good example paid off very handsomely.

Matsushita Konosuke did the same by cleaning a toilet no worker wanted to touch. With a pail of water and a mop, in the stunned presence of his workers, he completed the task. His workers have not forgotten this incident. They keep his factories meticulously clean, providing a pleasant working environment.

Spirit of Sharing

In setting examples for their employees to follow, executives like Matsushita and Sugimoto succeed because their employees know they are trusted. They have been taken into their bosses' confidence in the past and are willing to "win one for the Gipper." A remote American executive might enter his office with a pail of water and mop and make himself ridiculous just to provide comic relief to the daily routine. This is not so in well-managed Japanese companies.

In his younger days, Matsushita managed his own downtown

plant. A technical wizard of sorts, he unstintingly taught employees everything he knew. "Share everything with the men you can trust. They will never betray your trust and sell your secret," says Matsushita. "An important thing to remember is that you create a relationship of mutual trust." Iue Toshio, a brother-in-law of Matsushita, parted company with Matsushita to form his own company, Sanyo, in 1947. The same management philosophy of sharing and trust lives in Sanyo.[7]

Speaking of cleanliness, Sanyo creates a working environment that is as close to dust-free as possible for the production of electronic devices. Each morning workers coming to work at its TV, VCR or other plants remove their shoes, change into their slippers and wear the freshly laundered smocks provided by the company. At the entrance, mats are frequently changed to insure that no dust settles on them. Individually each of these steps may seem insignificant, but when all are observed carefully the workplace is transformed.

Office without Walls

A sense of sharing can be fostered when a top executive is willing to share an office with his subordinate in an arrangement we shall call "an office without walls."

Perhaps it is worth returning to the example of Hiroki, our typical management-bound employee climbing the corporate ladder. Throughout his working days, and at least until he becomes a *bucho* (division manager), Hiroki does not have a private office with a door he can close behind him. His work is done in an open office.

An average Japanese office is not well appointed. In a typical section, there may be eight desks, four in a row facing each other. The professional staff occupies these eight desks. The section chief's desk, slightly larger than the rest, may be placed nearby, standing alone or with that of a deputy chief. There is a little corner for a couch or two to receive visitors. OLs (office ladies), as they are called, with smaller desks and word processors constitute another island. The perennial tea pots and tea cups are placed near this group and everyone knows who must serve the tea.

In these surroundings, lack of privacy is well compensated by the camaraderie fostered in the office. Persons sitting next to and opposite Hiroki certainly know what he is doing and vice versa. In America, a call to a given section may be greeted with the answer, "Sorry, Jack is not in, and he is the only one who knows anything about this. Can he call you back at three?" In Japan this seldom happens. If a person is referred to a section, and if Hiroki who is in charge of that particular subject is at lunch, there is always someone else who can answer. They know each other's work well.

An open office without dividing walls has some disadvantages. It cannot insulate nonsmokers from being victimized by smokers, and it cannot control the unwanted noise decibel level, but the advantages far outweigh these inconveniences. The executive in charge of the office is always readily accessible to all.

At YKK, this practice has reached its logical conclusion, representing the ultimate in an office without walls. Adjacent to its Kurobe plant, a large building is converted into an office with no dividing walls. There are over one hundred desks arranged neatly into groups. In the center is a larger desk reserved for Yoshida Kyumatsu, the older brother of Tadao, who serves as Chairman of the Board. Once in the office, Yoshida is willing to meet with anyone who comes by, employees or visitors. His frequent presence in this office also conveys the powerful message that in YKK layers of management responsibilities cannot separate its top executives from employees. The company, after all, is just one big family!

On a much smaller scale, this concept of office without walls is efficiently applied at the JUSE press, the publishing arm of the Union of Japanese Scientists and Engineers. Its president and publisher, Mrs. Mitsuaki Haruko, sits in the middle of an editorial room with twenty other editors. Inquiries concerning their publications can be answered by any of the editors in the room. They communicate freely to each other in this office with no partitions. There is very little motion or time wasted. It is an appropriate setting for a publisher producing books on quality control and productivity.

Access to CEO

YKK has solved the issue of access to its top management through its office without walls. The question is, how can this concept be applied to the assembly line, where machines also regulate the flow of people? Musashi Seimitsu (precision) Industry Co., which makes parts for Ford and Honda (ball joint, crankshaft, gear, camshaft, and so on), has come up with an unusual solution. Each day for about an hour, its octogenarian president Otsuka Yoshiharu dons his white work jacket and cap and walks around the plant or office. Whenever he is wearing his cap and white jacket, anyone can stop him and speak to him. He loves to stop at different areas of the plant and operate machines alongside his workers. Once back in his business suit, however, he is not to be interrupted.

Sharing Corporate Values — Horizontally

The examples given above generally show vertical sharing of corporate values, as they are transmitted from one generation of employees to another, or from those above to those below. That, of course, is only one side of the coin. In Japan, a sense of belonging to the same corporation and sharing in similar corporate values is constantly reinforced by one's own peers. When employees work side by side in an office without walls, when performance is judged by group rather than by individual, and when compensation is based on seniority and ranking (*nenko joretsu*), those similarly situated tend to think and act alike. This tendency is further strengthened by lateral job rotation and socializing after hours.

Social gatherings are held frequently among company colleagues but seldom with outsiders. On payday, the entire section may go to a Japanese restaurant for a party lasting into the late evening hours. The stiff-upper-lip demeanor of the office is broken down. A normally reticent employee may find the courage to complain bitterly to his section chief or colleagues with the help of a few cups of *sake* and the appearance of being inebriated. The next day everything is forgotten and the office routine is resumed. Intended or not, these after-hours parties function as a safety valve, providing an outlet for the pent-up emotions of people who must work closely together for the rest of their professional lives. Companies encourage informal gatherings by sponsoring annual or semiannual overnight excursions for all employees. All expenses connected with these gatherings are paid by the company in return for the employees' goodwill. The bonds emerging from these gatherings are yet another way in which corporate culture is strengthened.

LABOR RELATIONS

The well-laid plan of managers and employees to create a viable corporate culture can come to naught if there is a hostile union. This has not been the case in Japan in recent years, however.

With West Germany, Japan boasts the best record in labor peace among industrialized nations. The unionization rate is substantially higher for Japan than in the United States. (In 1985, the rate stood at 28.9 percent, compared with 18.8 percent in the United States.) However, the number of days lost in labor disputes in 1985 was 257,000 for Japan as against 5,917,000 man-days for the United States.

Many factors have contributed to this phenomenon. Among them is the existence of companywide unions that tend to retain close identification with their own companies and are willing to participate in a joint effort to foster their distinctive corporate culture. It has not always been this way in Japan, however. In the 1950s, the possibility of powerful industrywide unions began to emerge in Japan. In the mid-1970s, after the first oil crisis, the worst nationwide wage disputes threatened the very base of cooperation that existed between labor and management. Remarkably, through it all, Japanese unions generally emerged not as adversaries but as independent agents in the creation of Japanese economic miracles.

Labor unions are generally organized companywide in Japan. In the hierarchy of values that an average line worker holds, he is a Mitsubishi or Nissan man first before being a member of a particular union. There are some industrywide unions more willing to resort to strikes and other means of protest, but their militancy has won few converts in recent years.

Odakyu

At Odakyu, a private railway company,[7] the union is a unique combination of company and industrywide unions, specifically, the Private Railway Workers Union established in 1947. The Odakyu workers' group became a member of this union the following year. Technically, the national union holds the right to negotiate with the industry representative on behalf of its 246 locals with regard to wages, bonuses, retirement pay and working conditions. However, a provision permits larger local unions, such as Odakyu, to negotiate with the company independently or alongside the national union. Thus, when the Odakyu local invokes this provision to assert its autonomy, it assumes characteristics that are much closer to those of a companywide union.[8]

There was a limited strike against the company by its office workers in March and April of 1958. At that time, working conditions at Odakyu were much worse than most other privately owned railways, and for that reason the local union asked the national union for permission to negotiate separately. From that time on, however, this practice became fixed and, while other locals struck, Odakyu never joined in but maintained their labor peace.

The 1958 strike resulted in the establishment of a number of committees designed to facilitate communication between the local union and management. These included committees on discipline, grievances, employee welfare and rationalization of management.[9] It was a modest beginning for a long-lasting company-union cooperation.

This does not mean there are no differences of opinion. Sometimes negotiations between the local union and the company can become very heated. The Odakyu local, however, does not believe in resorting to strike. "To strike means to divide the power and chain of command in the company into two, and that is not desirable," says local vice-president Sekino Fumio. "Instead of striking, giving a big financial headache to the company and inconveniencing our passengers, we prefer to establish an orderly system in which the lifetime employment system can be preserved."

The average age of Odakyu's 3,650 employees is thirty-eight. As the employees continue to age, the company has been tempted to remove them from employment in the name of rationalization. The union's tactic has been a simple one: they agree not to strike in return for the company's pledge to guarantee job security. This has worked well for both parties. The company and the union jointly maintain retirement counseling services to help retirees locate positions within Odakyu-related companies, find places to retire to and rearrange their financial affairs.

The Odakyu local enjoys a strong presence within the company. With the exception of 200 supervisors and executives, all employees belong to the union. The local is accepted as the sole bargaining agent by the company. A labor-management council meets regularly. Consisting of thirty-four members, evenly divided between management and labor, the council effectively provides both a sounding board and a safety valve. The management team is headed by the vice president. Unlike the United States, there is only one vice president in a Japanese company. The inclusion of the vice president in the council is positive proof of the company's determination to promote good labor relations.

The system for consultation developed by the company and the union is elaborate but not inflexible. There are standing committees and ad hoc committees. Over the years, the union has become a clearing house for grievances and has performed that task successfully. The company does not interfere in the proceedings of the grievance committee. If, however, a union member is dissatisfied with a committee decision, he has the right to appeal directly to the company president, provided the union is informed of this action.

The company and the union get along well. "They are a bunch of nice guys," says Koide Jutaro, a senior executive director, when referring to union leaders. "They are approachable and know our needs (*hanashi ga wakaru*)," says Oki Kenji, the local's secretary general, returning the compliment. There is no trace of antagonistic feelings between the two parties.

Antagonism in a companywide union is difficult to develop because all the principal players belong to "one big family." At Odakyu, once an employee reaches the executive rank he cannot remain a member of the union. Of the two hundred who are so excluded from union membership, however, many have been former members. Moreover, a stint as the union local president has often been considered a good step toward promotion into the executive rank. Many company negotiators have been former union officials. They are assigned to the negotiating table because they know the union well. They sit there not as the union's adversaries but as its friends and former officials.

Does this mean the union movement is a farce and that the union is merely a puppet of management? That is hardly the case. Certainly the Odakyu union fully accepts and respects the societal and public roles the company must perform as a transport company. The union is also willing to raise worker productivity in order to strengthen the company's financial base. In return, however, the union has been successful in asking for just compensation, better working conditions, and advance consultation when working conditions are to be changed. Working together as friends has been far better than as adversaries.

The union's positive contribution in the shaping of Odakyu's corporate culture is unmistakable. It prints a daily bulletin containing company and personal news. It holds meetings and seminars, and among the people who are younger, it creates effective peer support groups. If management has found its role in the shaping of corporate culture through a vertical route, what the union has done is to weave it with a horizontal approach. The warp and woof of a fabric called corporate culture are now firmly joined.

REFLECTIONS

Chrysler and Sanyo

The Odakyu example illustrates that both union and management can benefit when they work together as a team. This need not be a foreign concept to us in this country. When Chrysler went to Congress to ask for a federal loan guarantee, it also asked the UAW to share in the "equality of sacrifice." In the ensuing negotiations between the UAW and Chrysler, Lee Iacocca asked UAW's president, Douglas Fraser, to sit on Chrysler's board of directors. "He's had an enormous effect," says Iacocca, and here are his words:

> As a board member, Doug found out firsthand what was going on at Chrysler from the perspective of management. He learned how our suppliers contributed and that our turnaround wasn't only due to the workers. He learned that our profit-and-loss statements were real and that profit wasn't a dirty word. He learned and understood so much that some of the workers began to see him as a turncoat, because he told them the truth when we were too weak to take a strike.[10]

This represented participation by only one labor leader in management. What Odakyu has done, and many other Japanese companies are doing, is to allow a large number of their labor leaders to share in the management decision-making process. Given the effectiveness that Doug Fraser was able to show, the message of labor participation must not be lost.

Sohma Michitane, vice president of Sanyo in Forrest City, Arkansas, has this story to tell about its labor relations. In 1976, Sanyo purchased a plant in Forrest City from Warwick to establish the Sanyo Manufacturing Corporation (U.S.A.). Sanyo's president, Iue Kaoru, visited the plant to offer his congratulations. As is his custom at home in Osaka, he wore a work jacket with a name tag with his name IUE clearly printed on it. There was a round of applause as he entered the hall where the workers were assembled. A comment by a worker explained the enthusiasm with which he was greeted: "Isn't it nice! Our new boss is a member of the International Union of Electrical Workers!" Sanyo experienced a brief strike shortly after its Forrest City plant was opened. In 1985, there was another serious labor dispute. Otherwise, it has had a long period of labor peace. Perhaps Mr. Iue had helped his own cause by wearing the name tag IUE. The name tag aside, Sanyo's approach toward labor has been positive. As Sohma remarks, "We love labor unions. They help us." And this is in America!

Cooperation with Unions

Sharing responsibilities does not and must not mean yielding basic management prerogatives to the union, such as appointment of top executives or investment decisions requiring secrecy. Trouble occurs when this line is crossed. Shioji Ichiro, as president of Nissan's union until 1985, was in firm control of Nissan's personnel department and wielded enormous power. He guaranteed labor peace but at a cost too high for Nissan's management to pay. Men on the management track discovered that their promotions would not come without Shioji's assent. Ishihara Takashi, who became Nissan's president in 1977 and chairman in 1984, was heard to remark that he had to spend 70 to 80 percent of his time dealing with the union, meaning that he had to fight against Shioji's frequent interference. Shioji's hold on power came to an end when he openly challenged Ishihara's decision to establish a manufacturing plant in England.

The Nissan experience, however, is an exception to the rule in Japan. With his flamboyant personality, including owning and operating a yacht, Shioji exhibited characteristics which are considered "un-Japanese."

In companies like Odakyu, where hierarchy is respected and conformity is practiced, unions have worked well side by side with the companies. Grievances, when mishandled, can become inflammatory and politicized. The Odakyu union has excelled in its limited role of handling grievance procedures. By performing that function for the company, the Odakyu union has helped company management to become less politicized in performing its other duties.

Less Politicized Management

One impediment to good management experienced by American companies is politicization of the decision-making processes. Fear of destroying a carefully crafted political balance and the need to satisfy individual egos at various levels make change hard to come by. Innovative ideas have no soil to nurture them, because they must first be sold to someone higher up in the hierarchy as well as to those who must work on them. These restraining influences are minimized, if not eradicated, in the Japanese practices.

It is not necessary to dwell on the consensus-building mechanisms of *ringi* and *nemawashi*. The latter, in fact, can be considered a highly politicized activity by Japanese standards.

The Japanese system, however, encourages meshing of personal and corporate goals with individuals subordinating their ego for the greater good of the corporation. Corporate philosophies and annual policy goals reinforce these tendencies especially when they also contain superordinate goals. In formal and informal settings, the Japanese practices encourage dialogue between colleagues, sections, divisions, teams, superiors and subordinates.

In this chapter, the practice of "offices without walls" has been discussed. Figuratively, the phrase can also mean breaking down invisible walls of separation created by bureaucracy. The less bureaucracy, infighting and politicization, the better the chance for cross-fertilization and emergence of new ideas.

American managers who want to practice good management can apply some of the practices outlined in this chapter to ensure that employees will work toward the same goals. It is not cultural differences that make Japanese managers outperform their American counterparts. It is their use of a rational system of management, which incidentally can be transplanted with few modifications. Now here is our checklist:

Does our company have a corporate philosophy?

Is the language clear enough for the best educated as well as for the least educated?

Does the language mean the same thing to top management as it does to the line workers?

Are the goals simple enough to commit to memory?

Will I be happy with these provisions five years from now?

Do I use our corporate philosophy as a guide in my decision making?

When I have differing opinions about new projects, do I refer to our corporate philosophy?

Do I include superordinate goals my employees can identify with and be proud of?

Does my company supplement its corporate philosophy with annual policy goals?
- Do key personnel participate in the drafting of these goals?
- If each of our divisions also has annual goals, do the employees in these divisions participate in their drafting?
- Do we have an effective method of supporting cross-fertilization of ideas?
- Do we have an effective method of preventing overlapping of projects?

Do we have adequate methods of transmitting corporate values from one generation of employees to another, or from one group of employees to another (vertically as well as horizontally)?
- What are the formal methods we use?
- What are the informal methods we use?

Top executives are accessible to the following groups:
- Company directors
- Those above the rank of vice president
- Project managers on an ad hoc basis
- Office workers
- Line workers

Each month, at least once, have I asked myself this question: "How can the people who work for me have better access to me and receive my undivided attention?" Write down the answer for that month and implement it.
- My resolution
- Method of implementation

How recently have I praised my subordinates for excellence in their teamwork?
- If it is more than a month ago, have I somehow failed in making team assignments?

Finally, in what way have I contributed to the lateral dissemination of ideas to create a more congenial workplace for everyone?
- My contribution this month

After everything is said and done, gear yourself toward creating pride in your organization for yourself and your employees, because that is how a good team is formed. Emerging victorious in the Fiesta Bowl against the top-ranked Miami to claim the national title for his Penn State team in 1987, Coach Paterno remarked, "I am a great believer in the self-fulfilled destiny kind of thing. These guys literally made up their minds they were going to win a national championship. I don't know how you will it, but enough people got together and said they were going to do it and made the kind of commitment they made. There's no way I can tell you how much they inspired the coaching staff."[11]

D. J. Dozier, who scored the winning touchdown, was eighth in the voting for the Heisman Trophy and was chosen the offensive Most Valuable Player. Echoing his coach's sentiment, Dozier said, "(This MVP trophy) doesn't mean as much to me as winning the national championship. The team is first. We've always been that way." That is the essence of a good corporate culture. Incidentally, Penn State players' jerseys have on them the players' numbers but not their names. No Japanese team could have done better.

CHAPTER 4

Organizing for Productivity

In 1985, the United States had a current account deficit of about $50 billion against Japan. That figure was exceeded in 1986 by an additional $8 billion. The main U.S. imports from Japan were automobiles, iron and steel products, precision instruments, office machines, VCRs, TV and radio receivers and semiconductors, all of which (except VCRs) were once the exclusive domain of American industries. In numerical controls and robotics, another area of U.S. strength, Japanese companies made an impressive inroad into the U.S. market.

What has happened to the United States then? Pundits are fond of saying that the federal deficit, the resulting high interest rate and the strength of the U.S. dollar in 1985 and previous years are to blame. The September 1985 joint intervention initiated by Treasury Secretary James Baker and the finance ministers of Japan, Great Britain, West Germany and France brought down the value of the U.S. dollar by almost 40 percent against the Japanese yen. However, the basic orientation of U.S. trade with Japan has not changed.

As if bound by invisible fetters, the United States continues to purchase manufactured goods from Japan and to sell them raw material. Moreover, there is no prospect in sight to eliminate the huge current account deficit. Why? A simple answer for this phenomenon is that while Japanese companies have organized themselves to attain the highest productivity through continuous improvement, U.S. companies have faltered in their own efforts.

It is ironic. Two decades ago, America was still Japan's mentor in productivity. The Japan Productivity Center calculated that in 1967 the United States was three times as productive as Japan per man-hour. Giving Japan the value of 100, it cited the following U.S. figures in these areas for that year: automobiles, 496; precision machinery, 460; electrical machinery, 358; general machinery, 294; chemicals, 256; textiles, 237; and iron and steel, 204.

Today, the situation is reversed, though not in the same proportion. Japanese auto manufacturers on an average have a $1,200 cost advantage for each passenger car, but it is not as bad as the edge that the United States once had over Japan of five to one in productivity. It is still possible for U.S. industries to stage their comeback. To do so, however, they must first learn from Japanese practices.

Presented below are examples from Toyota, Mazda and Nippon Kokan, representing automobiles and steel, two of the three areas in which U.S. industries have found themselves most vulnerable. The third area, electric and electronic fields, will be discussed in a separate chapter. In all of these areas, productivity gains have come from Japanese companies' relentless pursuit of man-hour reduction, rationalization, and attention to quality. We shall begin with Toyota.

TOYOTA PRODUCTION SYSTEM

An economics professor from Pennsylvania visiting Japan for the first time commented after he saw Toyota, "I never realized how easy it is to make a car." Unwittingly he was coming to the heart of the Toyota production system. Machines whirled around the workers, but they never looked forbidding. The workers were surprisingly relaxed in going about their business.

The Toyota system, in the final analysis, is to make the process of manufacturing cars much easier and error free. By practicing this art, the company has been able to manufacture quality cars with competitive cost advantages.

Just-In-Time

Toyota is supported by just-in-time production and automation with a human touch. In an ideal manufacturing setting there is no waste in processing, equipment and personnel. To make the flow of things as close as possible to this ideal condition, Toyota has devised a system in which materials needed are obtained just-in-time, when needed and in the quantity needed.

The originator of this system is Ohno Taiichi, a former Toyota vice president, who received his inspiration from observing the working of an American supermarket. Here is Ohno's explanation of how the system works:

> Previously in every company, as soon as one process completed its work, its products were sent to the next process. In some instances, subsequent processes served as intermediate warehouses.... It was the responsibility of the process that manufactured parts and products to carry them to the next process. My thinking was that the responsibility for transporting should be given to the subsequent process.... As the subsequent process came to the preceding process to receive their materials, the preceding process had to replace whatever had just been transported. By adopting this method, intermediate storage areas became unnecessary. The preceding process manufactured what was needed and stored the item. Once the storage place was full, production had to stop.[1]

The subsequent process comes to the preceding process to withdraw the parts and materials it needs in the quantity it needs. The preceding process produces exactly the same quantity withdrawn. There is no waste involved, either in terms of excessive production or transportation.

At Toyota, the workplace does not receive anything resembling a production plan chart. It is not needed. Only final assembly is given a production plan showing which types of cars in what quantities are to be produced. The final assembly line goes to the preceding process to withdraw parts it needs, and the same procedure is applied to the one preceding that process, and so on. In this way, the system of withdrawal connects the manufacturing process in a series of chain-like links.

A *kanban* is used at each process to withdraw parts from the preceding process which in turn uses it to order production of parts. The word *kanban* means "a signpost." At Toyota, it is either a card or a sheet of paper encased in a plastic cover that provides all the information needed in withdrawing or ordering parts. The application of just-in-time, with the support of kanban, has resulted in significant management man-hour reduction. Another benefit is in the sharp reduction of unwanted parts. Toyota deliberately makes its storage areas small. Even in those areas assigned for storage, yellow lines are drawn. If anything goes beyond the line, it means storage has reached its capacity and production for that item must stop immediately.

Stopping the Line and Automation with a Human Touch

Conventional wisdom in the United States says that stopping the line is costly and that the decision should not be made by line workers. Toyota's thinking is totally different. If a worker cannot keep up with his assigned work, it is better that the production line is stopped. The foreman must reassess the assignments he gives. If defectives are produced, it is best to stop the line, so no mountain of defective products accumulates. If defectives are not detected and are sent to the subsequent process, costly repairs or even recalls can result. A cost-conscious manager will insist on correcting the situation on the spot.

Each process must discover the defectives it produces. The right to stop the line is merely one tool for that purpose. Stopping the line has a salutary effect on training employees. It gives the foreman and line workers a chance to get together to study current work procedures in order to prevent recurrence. A foreman who refuses to stop the line in the face of obvious difficulties is considered deficient in performing his duties. New employees are always taught how to stop the line. In fact, that is part of their first lesson.

Visual control is emphasized at Toyota, making the workplace easy to observe and manage. There is a stop button for every line. If for any reason the line is stopped, a display immediately appears on a board suspended above each line showing at which process in production trouble has occurred. This display board is called the *andon* (display lamp). Help can come instantly.

Machines are also "taught" to stop the line. Ohno calls this "automation with a human touch," and it means that machines are taught to behave like human beings. Assume that there is a high-performance machine and a foreign substance enters. The die is broken and maybe the tap. If production continues, defectives will mount up. Normally, a watchman is assigned to each machine to prevent this from happening. Once this is done, however, there is no longer any advantage to automation. Instead, an automatic stopping device is installed in each of the machines. When a foreign substance enters or when defectives are produced, the machine automatically stops. In concept, it is not different from a worker stopping an assembly line when he discovers that something is going wrong. The machine with a human touch can do the same with its automatic stopping device.

Load-Smoothing Production

Toyota's zeal in reducing excess capacity and inventory is relentless. Its goal is the attainment of zero inventory. If a manager accepts the challenge of reducing inventory, he is asked to be guided by the following process:

If you get to the one-half mark,
Cut the remainder in half, and
Cut the remainder in half again, and
Then cut the last remainder in half.

Effective utilization of existing capacity and implementation of the just-in-time system calls for a system of equalized production, balancing not only with the quantity but also the types of cars to be produced. At Toyota, this is called load smoothing.

Visitors to the Toyota assembly line are often puzzled to find that after a red Corona on the line, there may not be another red one until twenty other units are already assembled. Why is it that Toyota does not bunch all the red ones together and let them flow in sequence? The reason for this is that the types must be equalized.

If cars with red exteriors are placed on the assembly line to the exclusion of others, seats and other interior parts must also conform to the exterior color. It may make the work of assembly a little easier, but it may also create havoc among the preceding processes. One morning those who are producing seats and interior parts for red exteriors may require additional work, and in the afternoon there may be no need for their work. The determinant factor on the assembly line is the sales record for that particular time. If there are ten units of red and eight units of blue cars sold, then in that exact proportion, cars of these colors will appear on the assembly line. In this way, types can be equalized.

This concept of load smoothing is carried throughout the entire process, including stamping and other processes where dies must be exchanged. This otherwise cumbersome system, however, has not deterred Toyota from making load smoothing fully operational. It can now complete in three minutes the exchange of a die weighing 800 tons, a process that used to take three hours. Without this, the production of multiple types of cars in small lots would not have been possible.

Man-Hour Saving and "People Saving"

Just-in-time, automation with a human touch and load smoothing are three key concepts that have insured the success of the Toyota system. These concepts have limited application, however, for small- and medium-sized companies in other industries. Yet the Toyota system has been popular with them, especially after the first oil shock of 1973. It has been the belief of many industrial leaders in Japan that the Toyota system provides a sound framework for reducing man-hours and manpower, and shows the way for contracting company operations as well as expanding them. Here is another quote from Mr. Ohno:

"You have a labor-saving program and you reduce man-hours by 0.5 worker. Yet in reality, you have accomplished nothing. Only when you can reduce the number of actual workers involved, can you have a viable program of cost reduction. We must proceed to 'people saving' and not labor saving."[2]

It is a no-nonsense approach. Its basic assumption is simple: "Eliminate waste first." When excess time is discovered, do not be satisfied with the result. Redistribute work in such a way that all the man-hour savings can be bunched together into an equivalent of one man, and when that is accomplished, eliminate one person from the work force. Thus the work that previously required five persons may be adequately performed by four.

Perhaps a few words of explanation are necessary. Let us assume that there is a five-man work force. Worker A requires only 60 percent of the time allocated to him to complete his work. In the case of B, it is 80 percent; in the case of C, it is 70 percent, and in the case of D and E, it is 90 percent each. Among the five of them, there is 110 percent of time not effectively utilized when translated into one person's workload. In such a case, one worker can be removed from this group, and this is called "people saving" by Ohno. It is a useful concept for companies in time of contraction.

When a person is removed from the group, do you fire him? No, according to Ohno. What do you do with him then? Ohno reassigns him to another position, preferably in the same type of work. Now with the example given above, A is the best worker and D and E are the least efficient. When removing a worker from the group, which one does Ohno remove? The answer is A. The best and brightest must be removed. As good a worker as he is, A can improve the work process in the next station to which he is assigned, and the process of people saving can continue. Removing the best also has the salutary effect of informing everyone that good work does not go unnoticed. In contrast, if the worst were removed, the people-saving movement might be considered a form of punishment.

Incidentally, when a worker has no work to perform, he is taught to relax and do nothing. This will make it apparent that he has excess time on hand. It is a means of visual control that makes the next round of man-hour reduction and people-saving movement much easier to conduct.

The Workplace and the Foreman

At Toyota, the "standard operations" manual is drafted by the foreman in charge of the group to which the manual applies. It is not written by the engineering staff. The manual is used by the foreman as a tool for managing his group and teaching his workers. He is expected to work in accordance with the manual he has written, and if he finds it difficult to implement, he must revise it. This requirement also applies if workers in his group find the standards difficult to follow. In effect, everyone is asked to contribute to the manual of standard operations. It creates a feeling that management actually begins at the workplace. *Nemawashi*, that gardening term for consensus building, is practiced in the workplace in this manner.

The foreman serves his group more as mentor than as supervisor. He steps in to work with his group if someone is missing, and a sense of closeness is deliberately and deftly nurtured.

On employee relations, one additional fact needs to be mentioned. When a young man fresh out of high school enters Toyota's work force, he is usually placed in Toyota's dormitory for single men. He is assigned a person a year or two senior to him, who functions as his "older brother." Thus, the young man begins his apprenticeship in two ways. One is at the workplace itself and the other is at the dormitory under the tutelage of this "older brother." The company's values are transmitted to him through this one-to-one contact. It is a practice very much cherished in a company with close to sixty thousand employees, that ranks first in terms of profit and controls over 50 percent of domestic car sales.

MAZDA

Mazda's two plants, one in Hiroshima and the other at Hofu, provide two sharply contrasting images. The Hiroshima plant, where it all began, has an air of tradition and continuity. Formerly, all the company's operations were conducted in this one location. There were some super-craftsmen, such as those who once worked on Japan's mightiest warship Yamato in the nearby Kure naval shipyards. These super-craftsmen transmitted technical expertise to the next generation of workers, as if the latter were the former's apprentices. Workers had a sense of being part of one big family, even though the plant had grown in size. In spite of introduction of automation through the use of IBM computers, that sense of individualized craftsmanship persisted.

The opening of the Hofu plant on October 14, 1982, ended Mazda's fifty-one-year history of single location vehicle production in Hiroshima and ushered in a transformation in attitudes and the challenge of the new. Workers looked forward to the future, no longer harking back to the long-held tradition.

At Hofu, the four shops for stamping, body assembly, painting and final assembly are located close to each other in the so-called four-corner zone layout that facilitates communication among workers in different shops. At the body assembly shop,

130 robots do most of the spot welds on each car. At the paint shop, there are twenty-two robots applying sealers, undercoating and paint. After the paint is dry, doors are removed from the car body, each going its separate way to be fitted with parts before final assembly. The final assembly shop has a hanger-type assembly line tilted 30 degrees to allow workers to perform most of their underfloor work at eye level. The 1,800 workers, working in two shifts, can produce 20,000 passenger cars a month, 70 percent of which are for export. Cars are shipped directly from the pier next to the plant, which faces the Inland Sea. Although engines and some other parts are routed overland and subject to traffic congestion, all other parts of the operation have been totally rationalized to a tee. The plant functions with clockwork precision.

Total Productive Maintenance

In a highly automated plant like Hofu, maintenance is a critical issue. For this, the plant is guided by the total productive maintenance (TPM) concept already practiced in Hiroshima since December 1978. TPM activity has as its goal "total elimination of sudden breakdowns, little stoppages and defectives, to bring about 100 percent rate of operation." It emphasizes safety and inspection under the slogan "Inspecting in the morning for today, and inspecting before going home for tomorrow."

This movement is supported by six S's: *seiri, seiton, seiso, seiketsu, shitsuke* and *sense*.

Seiri means to put things in order, distinguishing between what is needed and not needed, and removing all items that are not needed.

Seiton means to keep everything in good order and ready for use. Workers are taught to make certain car parts or tools can be picked up efficiently when needed.

Seiso means to clean up everything properly. Workers are taught to remove all dust, dirt, scraps and foreign matter from plant facilities, machines, jigs, dies and inspection tools. They must maintain everything in such a way that the slightest imperfection in the machine or equipment can be readily detected.

Seiketsu means cleanliness. The working environment must be orderly (*seiri*), properly arranged (*seiton*) and properly cleaned (*seiso*).

Shitsuke means upbringing and inclination. Workers must be trained to be able to follow workplace regulations and work rules.

Sense is the English word used to means the innate sense or ability every worker must have to discern what is important and what is not. He must also be able to appreciate changes that are taking place around him.

When a Robot Is Not Needed

In Toyota's case, we learned that man-hour reduction must always lead to "people saving" to reduce the actual number of workers from a given line. Mazda does this, of course, and extends this concept to robots as well. Here is testimony from Yajima Kiyoshi, a foreman in the body assembly shop at the Hiroshima plant:

> My line handles the underbody for Mazda Luce and Cosmo. We used to have twenty-four robots with eighteen workers.... As we learned to use the robots, we discovered they were not utilized efficiently. The robots faced each other when doing the underbody welding. To avoid hitting each other, the robots had to take turns or have a period of waiting. We changed the placement of robots and the order of welding. In this way, we were able to reduce the number of robots from twenty-four to nineteen and the number of workers proportionately. At the same time, we discovered the cause factors for occasional stoppage and welding miss. Our quality improved and our productivity rose by 1.6 times.[3]

Like Toyota, both the Hofu and Hiroshima plants adopted the single-step exchange of die system. Also like Toyota, workers are allowed to stop the line. A refinement in the Hofu final assembly shop, however, divides the assembly line into three sections with buffer zones in between. Thus, stopping one section does not affect the operation of the other two sections.

QC for Subcontractors

A quality car cannot be produced without quality parts. Mazda has about two hundred parts suppliers who are predominantly small- and medium-sized family owned companies. With the memory of its serious mid-1970s setback with the Wankel engine and the accompanying loss of market share, Mazda embarked in 1977 on a massive quality educational program for its suppliers. It called this movement a "honeybee strategy." Just as a honeybee goes from flower to flower to pollinate, so quality can be transferred from company to supplier. Some "cooperating companies" or suppliers felt that Mazda was "putting the bee on" them to obtain more profit and refused to cooperate. In the end, however, ninety-one companies signed up.

The honeybee strategy called for Mazda to send three to four employees to the cooperating company for a period of three months. The employees sent were people knowledgeable in quality control, chosen from the industrial engineering and production technique divisions. They showed the cooperating companies how to rationalize their operations and taught them to utilize the methods of quality control. In a way, the honeybee strategy has been an extension of Mazda's own Mazda Quality (MQ) movement. As often is the case, practicing quality control has resulted in higher productivity for those cooperating companies.

NIPPON KOKAN, K.K.

Nippon Kokan is an integrated heavy industrial enterprise that incorporates steelmaking, shipbuilding and building of industrial plants. In steel production, it ranks second in Japan.

It has two integrated steelworks, one in Fukuyama by the Inland Sea and the other on Ohgishima, a man-made island in Tokyo Bay.

The Ohgishima plant sits on a 5.5 million square meter (6.58 million square yards) site. It is said that the land was reclaimed with 8.5 million cubic meters (11.1 million cubic yards) of earth, more than the amount dug to build the Suez Canal. The Ohgishima project was begun in 1971, in the days when Japan was still experiencing an annual double-digit increase in its GNP. The project was not completed until 1979, when the impact of the second oil crisis was fully felt.

Born of great hope to sustain the "iron age," it never showed its full potential as the demand for steel fell and the prices of fuel and raw materials rose sharply. In retrospect, the company would have done better if it had expanded its Fukuyama facilities instead of building a new one in Ohgishima. Yet Ohgishima remains the most modern, integrated steelworks anywhere in the world. Its presence reaffirms the company's commitment to steel and to the Kanto region where Nippon Kokan began its first operations. With its modern facilities, Ohgishima has enabled Nippon Kokan to remain competitive in the sluggish steel market.

Ohgishima has a number of distinguishing features:

1. All production facilities are arranged in a straight line running from east to west. From raw material unloading to product shipment, the intraworks transportation is fully rationalized.

2. The rate of continuous casting is above 90 percent, which is not only energy efficient but also insures stable, high-quality products.

3. On-line computer control is all pervasive, covering operations ranging from the receipt of orders to final shipment. The automated operation of production lines is fully computerized. The production lines affected include ironmaking, steelmaking, rolling through the plate mill, hot strip mill and seamless pipe mill.

4. Ohgishima is located in the Tokyo-Yokohama urban area. It has applied rigorous criteria in controlling air, water and noise pollution. About 20 percent of its estimated ¥1 trillion (about $3 billion at the then-existing exchange rate) building cost of the complex went to pollution control measures.

Nippon Kokan's Management Style

Nippon Kokan has been managed well. With the exception of fiscal years 1985 and 1986, when all steelmaking companies suffered losses due to the soft worldwide demand for steel and the rising value of the yen, the company has remained profitable. It has advanced its repayment schedule of debts. It has entered into the field of new materials and has been successful in cultivating its overseas market, with overseas sales reaching 41 percent and 31 percent in fiscal years 1985 and 1986, respectively.

The following are some of the characteristics of Nippon Kokan's management style:

1. Nippon Kokan was started in 1912 as a privately owned company and that tradition still survives. Unlike New Japan Steel, which was once owned by the government, Nippon Kokan shows a greater willingness to experiment and enter new fields. Like New Japan Steel, however, Nippon Kokan's management has a sense of community obligation and dedication to the national purpose.

2. While accepting a reduced amount of exports to the United States through various mechanisms applied by the United States, it has also been willing to join in partnership with American steel companies. One example is its purchase of a 50 percent share in National Steel in 1984 at the reported price of $290 million. This has also demonstrated Nippon Kokan's unshakable, and to some observers overly optimistic, belief in steel's future.

3. The company asks employees to "enrich your everyday life," and encourages them to use its many facilities, which in-

clude modern hospitals, hotels in resort areas, dormitories for single workers and apartments for married workers. All told, the company has invested heavily in employee welfare.

4. In making key decisions, employee welfare is always taken into consideration. The building cost per ton of crude steel produced annually is about ¥ 45,000 for Fukuyama and ¥ 170,000 for Ohgishima. In spite of this, the company went ahead with the Ohgishima project. An underlying reason for the company's action was that employees had been concentrated in the Yokohama-Kawasaki area working for the company's three older steelworks. Instead of transferring employees to other areas, the company chose to build a new plant at the site where these loyal employees could be absorbed. In this instance, cost became subordinate to employee welfare.

5. The company is fully committed to employee training and education. The level of discussion in employee meetings and quality circles is exceptionally high.

6. Employees have been willing to cooperate with the company in its rationalization measures. Both at Fukuyama and Ohgishima, before the two gigantic steelworks were built, an extensive *nemawashi* took place between the management and employees.

In times of adversity, Nippon Kokan has attempted to maintain its policy of not drastically reducing the number of its employees. It has preferred to retain most employees, with only a modest reduction registered through natural attrition. In 1985-86, it cut its work force above and beyond the normal attrition, but it did so with extreme reluctance, being the last of the major companies to take such steps.

Close yet Flexible Relations with Cooperating Companies

In Fukuyama especially, an elaborate system of cooperative companies has been developed to support every phase of the company's operation except administration and the direct act of steelmaking. One cooperating company provides attractively boxed lunches and dinners to employees at a subsidized price (about 40 percent of a comparable lunch or dinner). Another company unloads raw materials, while others handle fuel and the shipment of finished products. Some phases of the intraworks transportation are also handled by a cooperating company.

These cooperating companies are headed by individual entrepreneurs, by local businessmen or by former employees. They maintain autonomy but are given office space adjacent to the steelworks' central office to coordinate their business with the company and with each other.

The system of cooperating companies has served Nippon Kokan as well as the local economy. For the company, these cooperating companies provide an opportunity for those employees who want to retire because of age or inability to continue in the arduous steelmaking work. The pay scales for the cooperating companies are lower than in Nippon Kokan. When the latter enters into an agreement with the union or otherwise engages in wage adjustments, it can do so for its own employees only, without having to worry about the employees of cooperating companies who still provide essential services.

The operators of these cooperating companies are allowed to do business with other concerns besides Nippon Kokan. Their basic income comes from the work they perform for Nippon Kokan. Beyond this, however, they can venture out in the local economy, engaging in transportation, catering or whatever activity their specialization calls for.

The flexibility accorded by the cooperating companies is one of the reasons for Nippon Kokan's success in the competitive international market. Similar tales can be found in many other industries. The relationship between Toyota and its suppliers, discussed in the next section, is a prime example.

TOYOTA AND ITS SUPPLIERS

To build a Toyota Corolla, 3,000 parts are required, and if we add up each nut and bolt, the total will come to 30,000 pieces. Thus it is not difficult to see that managing parts suppliers becomes one of the most difficult problems in manufacturing a car.

At Toyota, supplies come from various sources, including companies within the Toyota group. They include Nippon Denso, the largest supplier of car electronics components, including air conditioners. Another supplier is Toyoda Gosei, which supplies plastics and rubber related parts, including dashboards, fan belts, window sealers and various hoses and pipes. Aside from supplying parts to Toyota, these Toyota group companies are encouraged to sell actively to rival companies. Nippon Denso was not named Toyoda Denso for this very reason. Toyoda Gosei sells to all of Toyota's domestic competitors except Nissan. The advantage to Toyota is obvious. Toyota gains economies of scale at a level much higher than that of its own parts requirements and saves the supplier's profit for the group.

If we treat products made by Toyota group companies as if Toyota made them, Toyota's approach to parts manufacturing resembles that of GM. At GM, the level of vertical integration is high, with about 70 percent of a car made in-house. This system was responsible for GM's high level of profit until the onset of the first oil crisis. There is one critical difference, however. GM is locked into this system by its contract with the United Auto Workers. It cannot suspend its production of parts when they are no longer profitable, and it cannot choose its own suppliers without union consent. The union contract may also hinder technological innovation, often regarded with suspicion by the union as a ploy to reduce manpower. These constraints do not apply at Toyota.

Parts suppliers rely exclusively on sales to car manufacturers. It is a buyer's market for the latter, and Toyota exploits this favorable condition to the hilt. It is not uncommon to hear small suppliers say: "I wish Toyota would share with us part of its huge profit," and "We are squeezed bone dry." They also complain about the added cost of storage until an order from Toyota comes to ship parts. As they term it, "We are victimized by their just-in-time program!"

Raw material suppliers do not fare much better. In the summer of 1977, New Japan Steel proposed a price hike per ton of cold-rolled strip of ¥6,900 or 8.7 percent. Toyota's opposition moderated its demand, and the final outcome was a price hike of ¥5,700 or 7.2 percent. It was the first time that the mighty steel had lost in price negotiations. One major steel company executive, who shall remain anonymous, confided to this writer, "These stingy characters. They never give you an inch."

Toyota and Matsushita

A story is told of Matsushita Konosuke's encounter with Toyota in 1961. Matsushita visited Matsushita Communication Industrial Company in Yokohama and was surprised that not one of its executives came to greet him. They were in conference arguing about the impossible demand just presented by Toyota that the price of car radios be dropped by 5 percent immediately and by another 15 percent six months later. At that time, net profit for each radio for Matsushita Communication was only 3 percent.

True to form, Konosuke gave an extraordinary answer:

> We lose 2 percent initially and then 17 percent, but I know Toyota has a good reason for asking. When liberalization of trade becomes a reality, automobiles must lower their cost by 20 to 30 percent in order to compete against foreign manufacturers.
>
> We only supply an insignificant part, but let us see this issue from our national perspective. We can either stop production of our color TV marked for export or accept Toyota's demand. When Japan's exports falter, there will be nothing left for us to produce. As an exporter, we must help another exporter. There is no other choice.

Change the design, but be sure not to lower the quality. Meet the price demand. Remember that I still demand that you come up with 10 percent profit.[4]

A year later, Matsushita was able to complete its design change and with rationalization made a 10 percent profit.

The story tells as much about Matsushita's way of doing business as it does of Toyota. Be that as it may, Toyota has been able to dictate terms to its suppliers. In September 1985, the joint currency intervention by five nations was announced, which attempted to lower the value of the U.S. dollar. Shortly thereafter, seeing that the intervention was working well, Toyota issued a directive to all of its suppliers. It demanded that the prices charged by them be lowered by 10 to 15 percent. It reasoned that the higher value of the Japanese yen was helping raw material manufacturers and parts suppliers by lowering their import costs, and that the step was necessary to make Toyota cars remain competitive in the U.S. market.

At about the same time, Matsushita and other home appliance manufacturers issued essentially the same demands to their suppliers. At the time these demands were issued, the exchange rate between the U.S. dollar and the Japanese yen was $1 to ¥206 or ¥207, with the value of the yen rising from the previous level of about $1 to ¥230 in September.

Toyota has been effective in guiding its suppliers to accept its technological innovation and improvement in quality. In this instance it does not necessarily dictate, but it has a strong power of persuasion. The approach used is similar to the honeybee strategy deployed by Mazda, and its weapon is quality control. Instructors in quality control are sent from Toyota to its suppliers to oversee or coordinate the latter's QC activities. In a two-way street approach, employees from the latter are invited to come to Toyota to receive their training also. By helping to train suppliers, Toyota also learns something in return. A bond of common dedication to quality is developed through these exchanges.

At Toyoda Gosei, the Toyota production system is effectively combined with TQC. Its employees can point with pride to the company's impressive record in quality assurance. Its brake lines, for example, are safe and Toyoda Gosei has not contributed to any recall of cars manufactured by its parent body or others in recent memory. Every worker knows how the parts he makes contribute to the car's performance and safety. Illustrations are posted on the hallways, walls and near the lines indicating how each of the parts manufactured there fits into a completed car. This phenomenon is not confined to Toyota, as the president of a company supplying parts to Mitsubishi can testify: "Our people may not drive a Mitsubishi-made car, but they know exactly how the parts they make fit into it."

The search for quality does not end at the level of immediate suppliers. Toyoda Gosei subcontracts parts and raw materials from other suppliers. The latter in turn receive guidance in QC from Toyoda Gosei. The cycle of quality assurance is thus complete.

REFLECTIONS

Toyota, Mazda and Nippon Kokan share a number of common characteristics in maintaining their fumble-free style of management:

1. They invest in rationalization. This includes investment in equipment and facilities and in organization, such as in the just-in-time system.

2. They invest heavily in employee training and education.

3. They are committed to quality, and QC circles are one means of attaining this goal.

4. They are export oriented and conscious of the events taking place around the world. The degree of their dependency

on exports in 1986 was as follows: Toyota, 47 percent; Mazda, 68 percent; and Nippon Kokan, 31 percent.

5. They have a system for controlling their suppliers without binding themselves, at the same time receiving the advantages of vertical integration.

What do all of these mean to American companies? As far as the just-in-time system is concerned, one must proceed with caution before deciding to adopt the system wholesale. It took Toyota ten years to perfect the system and it requires a lot more time and effort than most American firms are willing to invest in it.

We can still take to heart the basic assumption behind the Toyota production system, however, which is dedicated to the total elimination of waste — wherever it is found. Our immediate reaction is to ask, "How can we do it?" Under the Toyota system, probing into the cause is even more important than finding a solution. Before attempting to solve the problem, they ask "why?" five times, for instance, "Why did this happen?" "Why was this problem hidden from all of us?" and so on. If employees in our companies can get into the habit of asking five "whys" before attempting a solution — in Toyota's parlance "Five W's and One H (how)" — we have taken the first positive step toward competitiveness.

Relationship with Suppliers

Relations with suppliers and subcontractors have been thoroughly debated in Japan. Cost, quality and accumulation of technical know-how are among the factors that must be considered before deciding on whether to produce certain items and parts in-house or to purchase them from specialized manufacturers.

Dr. Ishikawa Kaoru, the noted authority on quality control, suggests that the following procedures be utilized when making a long-term commitment to subcontracting:[5]

1. Select a specialized manufacturer. In regard to the parts needed for your company, make clear which you want to purchase from this supplier, and which you want to produce yourself. A clear line of demarcation must be made from the outset.

2. Do you want your subcontractor (supplier) to become a specialized manufacturer who is independent and can supply products to other companies as well, or do you prefer to make the supplier into a subsidiary within your own industrial group? In that case, is your company willing to assume the burden of managing the subsidiary?

Management ability, especially in relation to quality control, is a key issue in choosing a supplier. The supplier must be familiar with the management philosophy of the purchaser and vice versa. The supplier's ability to maintain high technical standards and deal with future technological innovations must be thoroughly investigated. Of course, there must be a sense of mutual trust, and the supplier must pledge that no corporate secrets will be breached.

There is a saying that "the responsibility for quality assurance rests with the producer." In the supplier-purchaser relationship, it means that the supplier must be able to assure quality for its products. In Japan, where 70 percent of the manufacturing cost comes from outside suppliers, this is of critical importance. The ability of the suppliers to assure quality has been one of the key ingredients in providing Japanese companies with the competitive edge they enjoy in the overseas market.

The United States once had that edge and it is still not too late to stage a comeback. It may be a long and arduous task. U.S. companies may at first have to engage in 100 percent inspection and then gradually turn to sampling inspection before finally accepting parts and materials without inspection. To reach this final stage, the suppliers must fully meet the quality standards set by the company through its own process control. It means that the purchaser and supplier must work together over a long period of time. It may involve a period of trial and error, and relations can become strained. Only with determination and dedication can the two parties be able to bring this endeavor to a successful conclusion. Toyota, Mazda and Nippon Kokan have all demonstrated that such an undertaking is entirely possible. As an NBC special aired back in 1980 asks: "If Japan Can, Why Can't We?" Painful as it may seem, it is a lesson we must learn in rebuilding an industrial America.

Can a Domestic Content Bill Save Us?

From time to time, Congress has entertained the notion of passing the so-called domestic content bill, which would require that a substantial portion of a car sold in the United States be manufactured domestically. Its desire to protect jobs is understandable, but presently it would have net negative effects on U.S. auto manufacturers and ultimately on UAW's employment picture. Chrysler, for example, makes only about 30 percent of a car in-house. It shops anywhere for the best price and often its parts come from overseas. If this pattern were suddenly changed, Chrysler could lose much of the ground gained since its restructuring and recovery. It is not the fortune of one U.S. auto company, however, that is at issue. It is a matter of quality. When denied the ability to select the parts they need, auto manufacturers will not be able to assure themselves and their customers of the quality of the cars desired.

This statement, however, is not an endorsement of a practice that amounts to "offshore" production of part of an American car. American manufacturers have responsibility to their fellow Americans to retain jobs and skills in America. They must seek out American parts manufacturers and work closely together to improve quality and lower cost. They must ask themselves this one simple question: "If Japanese auto manufacturers that begin production of cars in the United States want their parts manufacturers also to enter the United States and begin production locally, why must we (the U.S. automakers) always seek our parts and materials overseas?" If the present trend continues, it might become possible to see American-made Japanese brand name cars competing in the U.S. domestic market against foreign-made American cars. For the public who wants to "buy American" where should their loyalty be? This is the specter American auto manufacturers must avoid at all cost. We cannot permit our industries to become hollow, and this task must be performed by American — not Japanese — managers.

GM's massive investment in new technology to cut manufacturing costs and Ford's and Chrysler's plant modernizations are movements in the right direction. It is hoped that this spirit of new adventure can be carried into the parts manufacturing sector. When informed of GM's investment in new technology and purchase of Hughes Aircraft, Toyoda Eiji commented, "This indeed is the reason why GM is to be feared. It will always remain a formidable competitor." Coming from this astute observer, it is a compliment. The auto industry does have a future.

The Steel Industry

The picture is bleak for the steel industry, however. The end of highway and school construction meant a slackening in demands for steel, which was further accentuated when the passenger car size became smaller. No serious facility investment has been made in the steel industry since the late 1950s, and the latest technological advances in steel seem to have passed America by. Even though the United States is self-sufficient in coal and can provide about 70 percent of iron ore domestically, that advantage is offset by the industry's higher transport cost.

Transportation cost is lowest in steelworks built by the sea, such as those in Japan. The once superior location in Pittsburgh at the confluence of the Allegheny and Ohio Rivers no longer provides advantages. Similarly, in energy cost, the U.S. rate is running at 144 against Japan's 100. The trigger price mechanism and other orderly marketing agreements cannot do much to revitalize the U.S. steel industry. These protective measures merely perpetuate inefficiency. Protection for a dwindling number of employees, without the industry's serious effort to reinvest and modernize, is an exercise in futility.

Nucor and other specialty steelmakers with electric arc furnaces are doing well. The issue the United States must be concerned with, however, is the survival of giant "integrated mills." Can America afford to lose them? What will its strategic consequences be? The consensus is that the nation desires to be strong. The nation may have its missiles and battleships, but in time of war can it be without some efficiently run integrated steel mills? The answer is, of course, no. Therefore, it is entirely reasonable to suggest that measures be adopted to encourage the revival of the steel industry in the United States. These measures may include tax incentives and protection against foreign imports for a limited period of time while the industry is engaged in rationalizing and modernizing its plants and management.

Back in 1955, a group of Japanese industrial leaders came to the United States to observe its steel industry. The group noted that productivity in the U.S. steel industry was high because:

1. The United States possessed rich iron and coal deposits.

2. The U.S. market for iron and steel was large and stable.

3. Specialization and standardization were the keys to the industry's ability to lower costs and increase profits.

4. Managers were imbued with the idea that high profits could be achieved only through an increase in production and decrease in price through free competition. Steelworkers knew that in order to maintain a high level of production, productivity would have to be increased, and they cooperated with management in attaining this goal.[6]

This report was read widely in Japan and became a basic text for steelmakers. What has happened to us since then? Perhaps if we all return to the basics — to the ideas held three decades ago — reaching there via Japan, we may yet regain our industrial prominence.

Now let us use our checklist to see what can be done in our industries:

Does your inventory system compare well with the Japanese system?
- Do you keep excess inventory?
- Is there a disparity in the inventory you keep for the manufacturing process and for the semi-manufacturing process?

If you have discovered that your inventory is excessive, have you asked yourself why?
- Has anyone else in your company asked the same question?

Toyota defines the term "lead time" as the time elapsed from the time it starts processing materials into products to the time it receives payment for them. Have you taken steps to shorten your lead time?

Does your plant have an adequate system of visual control?

Does your plant allow line workers to inspect their own work?

When these workers complete their own inspection, are the results given promptly to their foreman?

Can engineers and line workers work side by side in your plant?

Your union contract may not allow non-unionized workers to be on the shop floor working side by side with union members. If you have such a provision, place that on the agenda for renegotiation. Breaking down the wall of separation between line workers and engineers is one of the most important steps toward achieving higher productivity.

The following checklist is designed primarily to test your relations with your subcontractors. It may be used inwardly, however, to judge your own company's performance.

Does your intended subcontractor have a corporate philosophy containing values compatible with yours?

Is the subcontractor's management stable?

Are the technical standards maintained by the subcontractor consistent with your own?

Does the subcontractor show willingness to accept technological innovations you may suggest?

Is the subcontractor willing to establish its own total quality control program?

Can the subcontractor meet the date of delivery in the amount desired?

CHAPTER 5

Quality First

Karatsu Hajime of Matsushita and R. W. Anderson of Hewlett-Packard met at a joint U.S.-Japan "Seminar on Semiconductors" in March 1980 in Washington, D.C. There the two discussed the relative merits of semiconductors in the United States and Japan. As Karatsu reported, products from three U.S. manufacturers and three Japanese manufacturers were compared side by side and the following results emerged:[1]

Manufacturer	Checking Inspection	Failure Rate per 1000 hours	Quality Evaluation
Japanese Co. I	0	0.01	89.9
Japanese Co. II	0	0.019	87.2
Japanese Co. III	0	0.012	87.2
American Co. I	0.19	0.09	86.1
American Co. II	0.11	0.059	63.3
American Co. III	0.19	0.267	48.1

It was three to nothing in favor of Japan, and this was in 1980 when American semiconductor manufacturers were fully confident that this was one frontier no Japanese manufacturers could penetrate. Quality and reliability were on the side of the

Japanese, however. Within a few years, Japanese semiconductors captured the U.S. market and by 1984, U.S. makers were experiencing a slump. Diligence in observing quality control had paid handsome dividends for its practitioners.

What is ironic is that quality control (QC) is an American invention. It was begun by Dr. W. A. Shewhart of Bell Laboratories in the 1930s when he made an industrial application of the control chart. In 1950, Dr. W. Edwards Deming went to Japan to give the first series of his remarkable lectures on statistical quality control. The idea spread across the country, and to paraphrase a familiar American expression, QC became as Japanese as cherry blossoms. Quality first is an article of faith among Japanese companies and, to any one of them, receiving the Deming application prize in quality control is the ultimate in peer recognition.

WHAT IS QUALITY CONTROL

The Japanese Industrial Standards (JIS) define quality control as follows:

> A system of production methods that economically produces quality goods or services meeting the requirements of consumers. Modern quality control utilizes statistical methods and is often called statistical quality control.[2]

Dr. Ishikawa Kaoru redefines the term as follows:

> To practice quality control is to develop, design, produce and service a quality product which is most economical, most useful and always satisfactory to the consumer.[3]

To fulfill this goal, everyone in the company must participate. This companywide participation is often called companywide quality control (CWQC) or total quality control (TQC). A customer orientation is preferred over producer orientation. This is also expressed as "market in" rather than "product out." Customers must *always* be satisfied.

This concept of customer orientation is extended to the manufacturing processes. Dr. Ishikawa is fond of saying that "the next process is your customer," and tells the following story:

> We were trying to work out a solution to the problem of reducing the number of defects and scratches in steel plate at a steel mill one day in 1950, and the following exchange took place:
>
> Ishikawa: Why not call in the workers in the process next to yours and the one before yours to investigate?
>
> Process manager: Professor, do you mean to say we should call in our enemies?
>
> Ishikawa: Wait a minute. The next process should be your customer. Why do you call them enemies? Every evening go to the plate mill that is your next process and ask, "Are those ingots we delivered today satisfactory?" That should create better relations.
>
> Process manager: Professor, we can never do that. If we go to the next process unannounced, they will think we are spying on them. They will immediately chase us out.[4]

This is a scene all too familiar in many industrial countries. In Japan, thanks to the efforts of Dr. Ishikawa and others, this kind of sectionalism is fast disappearing. One of the positive effects of quality control is its ability to break down the walls of sectionalism and bring in a breath of fresh air.

QC Circle

When a company begins a quality control movement, it encourages its employees to form their own separate quality control circles. Participation, however, is strictly voluntary.

The Japanese Union of Scientists and Engineers (JUSE), which serves as the secretariat for all QC circle activities, provides the following definition for the QC circle. The version quoted is JUSE's own English translation, printed in the manner it is presented by JUSE.[5]

What is the QC circle? The QC circle is
- a small group
- to perform quality control activities
- voluntarily
- within the same workshop.

This small group carries on
- continuously
- as a part of companywide quality control activities
- self-development and mutual development
- control and improvement within the workshop
- utilizing quality control techniques
- with all the members participating.

QC Story

Members participating in the circle are taught basic statistical methods called the seven tools of QC. They are taught to speak with facts and data, not with hearsay evidence. In making presentations, they generally follow the outline given below, which is called the QC story.[6]

1. Deciding on a theme (establishing goals).

2. Clarifying the reasons this particular theme is chosen.

3. Assessing the present situation.

4. Analysis (probing into the causes).

5. Establishing corrective measures and implementing them.

6. Evaluating the results.

7. Standardization, preventing slip-ups and recurrence.

8. Afterthought and reflection, considering remaining problems.

9. Planning for the future.

The QC story is a useful tool, providing uniformity in making presentations. It also helps prevent misstatements, resulting in miscues and miscommunication.

SOLVING PROBLEMS WITH QC

QC is an effective problem solver and Japanese companies have utilized it to enhance their own productivity and competitiveness. In the absence of QC, of course, problems can still be solved. With QC, however, problems can be more easily and accurately identified and actions to be taken can be standardized. The result is greater efficiency.

The control circle of "plan-do-check-action" (PDCA) aids in problem identification and action implementation. The *plan* and *do* parts are further subdivided into the following six steps:

1. Determine goals and targets.

2. Determine methods of reaching goals.

3. Engage in education and training.

4. Implement work.

5. Check the effects of implementation.

6. Take appropriate action.

Problems besetting a company are the result of a variety of cause factors. To be able to solve a problem, these cause factors must be identified. Among these cause factors, however, some are truly important while others are not. QC utilizes statistical tools, such as the Pareto chart, to standardize the two or three most important cause factors and control them. In searching for these cause factors, people familiar with the process such as line workers and engineers are always consulted. One of the strengths of QC, in fact, lies in this broadly based participation.

To illustrate how QC works, some common problems facing both U.S. and Japanese companies are given below. To each of them, a solution by a Japanese company using QC methods is given. Before you read the solutions, however, please formulate in your mind how you would react to each of the problems presented. By knowing the difference in your own approach from that of your Japanese counterpart, you may find one of the keys in unlocking the secrets of Japanese productivity.

PROBLEM 1: The Paper Workload

No matter how fast you read the memos in your in-basket, by the end of the day you still have twenty or thirty of them left. You stay late and finish reading them. Next morning you start afresh, but by the end of the day, you still have another pile of twenty or thirty. This goes on every day, and there is no end in sight.

It is true that memos are needed to make the office function, but they do not seem to do what is intended. You can remember asking the maintenance department to fix your telephone extension, and twice sending your work order in triplicate. Nothing has been done. You asked your superior about an important personnel decision; again a memo from you was required in triplicate giving your rationale. That memo is perhaps still sitting on your director's desk and, of course, nothing has been done. You had this splendid idea on marketing initiative, and again market survey, rationale, and so forth, all in triplicate, were required. Three months after your initial submission, however, no one has said a thing about it. In the meantime, your bosses, colleagues and those who work for you keep sending you memos.

It is very frustrating, but the work of the office goes on....

Questioning the Problem

How can QC help solve this problem? Let us begin by using Toyota's "five W's and one H" formula by asking "Why?" five times first. Why am I writing this memo? Why am I sending this memo to Mr. X? Why am I submitting this memo in triplicate? Why am I reading this memo (do I really have to)? Why do we insist on exchanging memos? By the time you come to the fifth question, it becomes obvious that the problem cannot be solved by yourself alone. It also becomes clear to you that you need a QC circle to iron out these common problems. In any event, ask as many questions as are necessary to find a solution, always starting your question with a "why." After you have exhausted the whys, you can proceed to ask: "How can I solve this problem?"

You may come up with Procter and Gamble's one-page memo as a solution. Why then does your company insist on multi-page memos, and why do you slavishly follow that practice? "Well, my boss likes it that way," you may rationalize, "and it makes me look good." The key issue is this: "Does it help my company increase its productivity?"

David Brinkley commented on a network news program once that to reduce the heavy workload in the government, it should be decreed that all correspondence be done on a small-size sheet of paper. He jokingly suggested that we cut our regular 8½ x 11 inch sheet into four pieces, and use each piece as our basic means of written communication. No one took him seriously.

Pentel's Solution

The illustration below is a replica of Pentel's office memo form, reproduced in the exact size. It is a little wider in width but a shade shorter in length than a normal business card. To the side of the original Pentel form, parallel to the Japanese writings as printed, the English counterparts are given:

BUSINESS MEMO	Date of request	Yr.	Mo.	Day	Hour
	Date Promised	Yr.	Mo.	Day	Hour
To be reported to:		Requested of:			

As can be seen, there are only five lines on which a message can be written. The back is not to be used.

Assume that a Pentel employee meets the company's managing director and suggests something to him. Instead of waiting until he returns to his office, the employee summarizes his idea in five lines and presents that to the managing director, using this memo form. Conversely, if the managing director wants this employee or other employees to engage in some specific tasks, he communicates his desire by using this memo. All Pentel employees carry a supply of these memo forms along with their green-covered appointment books. When they meet for a conference, the blank memo forms are immediately put on the table. As the meeting progresses, the participants note whatever tasks they want others to perform on the blank forms and exchange them freely among themselves.

Initially, when a sender wrote a memo, the original was given to the recipient, and the sender did not retain a copy. An OL (the term frequently used by the Japanese to indicate an office lady) came upon a suggestion at a QC circle that the blank memo form should always have two copies pasted together with carbon backing on the first. So now both sender and recipient have a copy.

The memo encourages making decisions quickly, often on the spot. When a request is received, priority must be given to that task. In principle, all tasks ordered or requested must be completed within twenty-four hours. If more time is needed, the recipient must report that fact, usually in writing, to his superior and the sender of the memo.

When a task is completed, the recipient sends a summary of the five-line memo in writing to his superior. The receiver's copy is returned to the sender to indicate completion. The sender may then destroy both copies of the memo, completing the cycle.

Pentel holds frequent employee meetings, creating an atmosphere in which face-to-face discussions are valued more highly than excessive written communication. If a task has not been completed, the subject may be raised at one of their meetings or privately with the sender. There are no specific rules governing all contingencies. The overriding consideration is how to get the work done well and quickly. Paperwork must not stand in the way of real work. It is as simple as that.

Pentel was started in 1946 as a modest stationery store but it now has eleven subsidiaries overseas in addition to a network of sales organizations and three manufacturing plants in Japan. It sells felt-tip pens, ceramic-tip pens, water-based ball-point pens, crayons, pastels and other materials for drawing and painting, school and office suppliers, and office machines, including *kanji* electronic typewriters. It attributes its success to quality and to its closeness to customers. Its founder and president, Horie Sachio, visits his subsidiaries worldwide. On overseas trips, he visits customers to get their reactions to his products. He makes good use of his own business memo forms by writing memos to himself and on his return trying to complete the tasks within twenty-four hours! This is not always possible, of course, but in this manner, he and others in the company are continuously introducing new ideas.

PROBLEM 2: When Imports
Threaten Your Company's Existence

Your company is in trouble. For the past five years, your profit
has steadily declined. Foreign imports have seriously under-
mined your market position. What was once securely yours, you
can no longer take for granted. Your foreign competitors have
the advantage of newer plants and equipment. With their rising
sales, they also have economies of scale you do not enjoy. Your
old customers may still buy from you out of friendship, but they
also complain that your products do not measure up to the
foreign imports. Your options are limited.

Does this sound familiar? Before you go on, pause for a moment
and consider the options. You may think that the Chapter 11
bankruptcy option looks attractive. It allows you to continue
operating your company and get rid of the nasty union contract. Or you may want to shut down some of your plants to save
costs, or relocate your manufacturing plant to Mexico or
Taiwan to take advantage of cheaper labor costs, and so forth.
Another option is to import cheap foreign products and sell
them under your own brand name. Whatever you choose, some
of your employees are going to lose their jobs.

Komatsu's Solution

The scenario above may suggest the all-too-familiar plight of
American companies. Similar conditions happened in Japan,
however, in the early 1960s.

Economists generally assign 1955 as the year when Japan's
postwar economy took off and began its spectacular growth. In
those days, however, an air of uncertainty persisted. The 1956
edition of the *Economic White Paper* began with an instant catch
phrase, "The postwar era is over." At the same time, however,
it cautioned that "growth through recovery is over. Hereafter
economic growth must be sustained by modernization." For Japan

to continue its growth, it required infusion of foreign technology, and that meant technology from the United States.

In the year 1961, Caterpillar, then the world's largest construction equipment manufacturer, announced that it was going to establish a joint venture in Japan. It was a means of introducing technology to Japan and the move was welcomed by the Japanese government. Komatsu, Japan's major manufacturer of construction equipment but far smaller in scale than Caterpillar, felt threatened. The Japanese government's position was that the policy of liberalization ought to be pursued, leaving few options for Komatsu. However, Komatsu decided to fight back, and the weapon they chose was quality control.

Komatsu's management knew that without quality there could be no survival for the company. It drafted a policy statement, called Project A, whose purpose was "to improve the quality of medium-sized bulldozers to the level of competing machines within a short period." To do so, it was necessary to disregard cost and Japanese industrial standards (JIS). It meant that Komatsu would set much higher standards for itself in order to be able to compete effectively in the world arena. Time was of the essence, and only medium-sized bulldozers were chosen as the ones on which the company was to stake its survival and challenge the mighty Caterpillar.

Kawai Ryoichi was a senior executive director at that time. He knew Dr. Ishikawa Kaoru, his tennis companion in high school days. Ishikawa came to help, and Kawai was made vice-president to coordinate the QC activities. As Kawai can recall, it was a desperate move on the part of the company, "grasping at straws," so to speak.

QC teams were quickly formed to receive instruction from Ishikawa. The latter's first question was: "Who knows Komatsu's products best?" The QC teams answered almost in unison: "Our design engineers." "No," Ishikawa thundered back, "it's your customers." Komatsu's challenge to quality was thus begun.

The first order of business for these teams was to compile information received through customer complaints. Visits were made to customers. Field surveys were conducted by territory, operation condition and soil condition. Actual overhaul records were carefully studied and data from competitors added to this study. Durability of parts, like the track shoe, was carefully investigated. Repair records kept by dealers were examined and comments from servicemen were carefully analyzed. With these data, the QC teams had something to go on. There were 1,839 cases assembled that pointed out problems existing in Komatsu's medium-sized bulldozers.

As these data were studied, the QC teams suggested that the plant initiate a program to reduce defects by half. The plant manager, however, could only set the target at a 30 percent reduction. At this juncture, reorganization of the QC teams took place.

At Komatsu, due to the emergency nature of the QC project, QC teams were organized only among management personnel initially, and QC activities appeared to follow a "top down" rather than the more favorable "bottom up" approach. This was to change immediately, and by 1963, opportunities to participate in QC circles were widely available. Although there was no compulsion from the top, a shared sense of crisis encouraged line workers to sign up for QC circle activities in droves. The circles often set their own goals but, in setting them, they also became familiar with company goals. These circles were the ones that would suggest adding an additional 5 percent to the 30 percent reduction goal already proposed by the plant manager.

Within a year, Project A was completed, meeting its goal of attaining a 50 percent reduction in defectives. Durability of products doubled and the company was able to raise its period of guarantee from 300 to 600 hours. A new product development system became fully integrated with QC at this time.

In new product development, evaluation followed each of the steps of planning, development, preparation for manufacturing and sales, and production. The first evaluation examined the product to see if it met customer needs. The next examined the prototype to see if it was fully developed in accordance with the standards set. The following evaluation checked the product's durability half a year after its manufacture, subjecting it to a 600-hour durability test. When these tests were completed, actual production began.

Evaluation following actual production was conducted between six months and a year after the customer purchased the product. Company employees visited customers to subject the heavy earth-moving machines to performance tests. The next lot production would begin only if the tests proved satisfactory. At each of these steps, QC became a vital link to quality. To confirm the results of the quality improvement plan, the company manufactured ninety-six experimental bulldozers, testing them under continuous operation.

By 1972, Komatsu felt confident enough to start building large-size bulldozers, always using Caterpillar products as the challenge to be met. Export sales became an important factor in the company's profit in 1975. The following year there was a decline, but in 1980, export sales rose sharply with a continuous increase ever since. In overseas sales, Komatsu's price has always been set at 5 percent below the competitor's. In the service area, the company has announced that it can go anywhere in the world within forty-eight hours. Today Komatsu is a top competitor of Caterpillar.

In retrospect, the crisis experienced in 1961 had a salutary effect on the company. Crisis brought management and labor closer together, and the company made a long-range commitment to raise quality through the application of QC. It taught employees the importance of customers. Quality became their sole weapon in fighting a foreign giant. The company subordinated profit to a higher cause and thus secured the unqualified support of its workers. Through QC, workers knew that what they said and did counted. It was a very successful case of QC application.

PROBLEM 3: Complacency

"Last year was another outstanding one for our company. Profits were the second highest in the firm's forty-eight-year history. Net income for the year ending December 31, 19__, was...."

How would you react to a statement like this from your company? Would you be thinking in terms of the value of your stock options or a sizable bonus increase? Or would you consider investing in plant and facilities or lowering product prices for a higher market share?

Actually, when your company is doing well it is time to be doubly cautious. Your company's good fortune may be due to luck more than anything else. As a manager, you may become careless and begin to believe in your own invincibility; you lose your critical power of observation. Self-indulgence is one of growth's worst enemies. As they say, "What goes up must come down." Your company cannot remain at the pinnacle if managers like yourself become complacent.

"The company is eternal (*kigyo wa eien nari*)," some Japanese executives say. However, Nikkei Business, a research arm of the *Japan Economic Journal*, has a sober note and warning: The life expectancy of a company is only thirty years. [7] Nikkei Business bases this statement on its study of companies included in the lists of the top one hundred companies compiled in 1896, 1911, 1923, 1933, 1943, 1950, 1960, 1972 and 1982. Only one company (Oji Paper) consistently made all the lists. Even the mighty Kanebo, which was the top-ranked company in the 1896, 1923 and 1933 lists and which never left its position as one of the five largest companies in Japan through 1960, did not make the list in 1982. Many famous companies of the past are today only names in the memories of corporate historians.

Toyoda Gosei

To executives intent on rescuing their companies from complacency, QC provides an ideal weapon.

When Nemoto Masao became president of Toyoda Gosei in 1982, he inherited a company that was well managed. Its pre-tax profits rose by 26 percent within a two-year period. Its efforts for rationalization, coupled with its aggressive stand in securing new markets including those overseas, seemed to be paying rich dividends. There had not been a single instance of recall of cars resulting from poor parts supplied by Toyoda Gosei since 1980. Its defects were measured in PPM (parts per million). Some employees felt that the company was as good as any in the world among those manufacturing rubber and plastic products. To free its employees from this attitude of complacency, Nemoto chose quality control.

To Nemoto, who had had rich experiences both in total quality control and in the Toyota production system, this new assignment at Toyoda Gosei provided an unusual opportunity to combine the two systems. He wanted to pose this as a challenge both to himself and to the company. He also wanted to use QC as a means of educating his employees, especially those in middle management. Many of his section chiefs came from engineering backgrounds. As they advanced in rank and responsibility, however, there was a need for increased managerial awareness and capability. QC could give exposure to and training in these areas. The stage was set for Toyoda Gosei to go full force for quality control, which culminated in its being awarded the Deming application prize for 1985.

"Go to the next division, ask them how they feel about your work and actively solicit their complaints," was Nemoto's first instruction to his executives. He wanted to break down the walls separating the divisions. He wanted them to be honest with themselves and with each other. In order to improve, one must know where the problems are; there is no better way to find the problems than to ask those who are affected by one's own work. Soliciting complaints was for that purpose. Once the practice was formally instituted, it was surprisingly easy to continue. Instead of "how dare you say such a thing," most executives responded, "Thanks, I didn't realize what I was doing." A by-product of this practice was a significant improvement in interdivisional communication.

One of QC's fundamental principles is to go to the source. Quality must be built into the product and, to do so, it must begin at the design stage. When design changes are to be made, however, does it mean that quality becomes the exclusive domain of the engineers? The answer is no, of course. At Toyoda Gosei, engineers are asked to go to the workplace, pick up the piece for which they are to make the design change, discuss all pertinent issues with line workers and work alongside them to get a feel for the product. No designing or change can be made in abstract in the laboratory.

The educational effort in QC is intense but not overwhelming. The practice of "one point QC," for example, focuses on only one thing at a time. Normally, it utilizes a cartoon to explain a point. In one example, a metal clamp, magnified several times its actual size, appears in the center. A bare hand is shown about to touch the clamp. Across the top of the hand is a big X or "no-no" sign. To the left is a one-sentence explanation: "Because it will cause rusting." Above the picture is this admonition: "Don't touch the product with your bare hand." Below the picture is the "how-to" column: "Always use a gloved hand." There is space for entry by the initiator of the lesson with his signature and date. Anyone who has seen the poster and agrees to abide by that particular lesson affixes his signature and the date.

The Haruhi plant, which has a 50 percent share of brake lines in the domestic market, has converted its large-lot system of production into the multi-types small-lot system of production. Foolproof and failsafe devices are incorporated into all processes. Sensory inspection is quantified and mechanized to enable workers to discover abnormalities and take necessary corrective actions as early as possible. The Toyota production system's simultaneous one-piece flow production system is the pattern governing each process.

The Haruhi plant has impressed visitors with its essentially odor-free environment. The peculiar odor that comes from a factory using rubber is conspicuously absent. Small lamps and boards, with the *andon* system of visual control are very much in evidence. Lines stop automatically when defectives are found. Machines are clustered so a worker can handle five or six of them sequentially. The Toyota system works well there.

In one of the lines, the lead time — that is the period of time between planning and completed manufacture of a product — has been cut from 4.4 hours to twelve minutes. In this line the number of workers was reduced from seven to three and then to one. As for defectives, the incidence began falling in 1983 and by April 1985 it attained 67 PPM (parts per million). QC has proven an excellent tool in raising productivity and profits.

IBM Japan

IBM Japan calls its quality control program CS activities. CS stands for customer satisfaction, indicating IBM's commitment to the philosophy of "market in" or customer first. The goals are "people development, strengthening the organizational structure through CS activities and teamwork." CS activities have taken Shiina Takeo, its president, to its divisions, departments, plants, laboratories and sales organizations to audit the effectiveness of QC activities, or merely to participate in one of the circles.

The example set by Shiina has been emulated by his directors who have taken an active part in the presidential or divisional audit and other QC activities. It has fostered a sense of belonging in a manner not previously apparent in this company of close to 17,000 employees. As former CS activities division leader Morita Shintaro remarked, "It's not every day that employees can meet the president face to face, but through participation in QC they receive unusual opportunities."

In June 1982, FBI agents arrested six Japanese on the West Coast for industrial spying against IBM. In spite of the fact that IBM Japan was not involved, it created an almost impossible situation for the company. In Japan there were demonstrations against IBM decrying the unfairness of entrapping hard-working Japanese businessmen. Death threats were uttered by some extremist groups against key IBM Japan executives. They wanted these executives to "go home to the United States," even though all of them were Japanese nationals. IBM Japan employees, however, remained loyal to the company. In this period of uncertainty and identity crisis, QC activities provided the glue that bound the employees together.

Incidentally, for three years in a row, between 1983 and 1985, IBM Japan experienced double digit growth, and in 1984 it was 25.6 percent over the previous year. The figure for 1985 was somewhat more modest at 19 percent, but it was accompanied by a vastly improved profit picture. In 1985 and 1986, it hired a large number of new systems engineers to strengthen its customer service activities and continued to grow in spite of the worldwide slump in the computer market. Shiina's comment is "not to be content with our present success and to make an all-out effort to achieve still higher goals." That is consistent with Nemoto's "improvement after improvement" philosophy, and both are in the best tradition of QC activities.

PROBLEM 4: Unevenness in Performance

Your division X performs consistently. It is not spectacular but every year it brings in good profits. Division Y is uneven, combining a dismal record with an almost inexplicably strong record from one year to another. Division Z has been a poor performer.

You have done everything you can. You have tried to shake

up the division personnel. You sent the head of Division X to Y hoping that he might reshape the division into a consistent performer, but you ended up having two years of consistently miserable performance at Division Y. You cut some of the poor performers' executive perquisites but only received complaints in return. What else can you do?

In desperation you have thought of a wholesale firing, but a mere personnel shakeup probably would not do much good....

Matsushita — Division as Independent Enterprise

Matsushita solved a similar problem by making each of its divisions an independent operating unit. For the purpose of accounting, each division is "an independent enterprise" with its own "internal capital" consisting of fixed assets and operating capital initially provided by Matsushita's head office. All operating decisions, including administration, marketing, purchasing, manufacturing and personnel, are to be made by the "independent" division. The price of this "independence" is a steep one, however. In return for the rights thus granted, the divisions must meet the following conditions:[8]

1. All divisions must secure a 10 percent profit before tax relative to sales. Divisions must also pay 10 percent interest on the "internal capital" granted by the Matsushita head office.

2. Generally, each division may retain 40 percent of its profit before tax, which may be kept as its internal reserve. The head office uses its 60 percent share for paying dividends, paying taxes and creating its own internal reserve.

3. Divisions may borrow from the head office at a rate consistent with bank loans. If the loan amount exceeds the amount permitted for that particular division, a penalty rate will be assessed. No division is permitted to borrow directly from commercial banks.

4. The principle of cash-only transactions must be honored.

5. All divisions are ranked in three categories: "A" with a

profit before tax of more than 10 percent; "B" with more than 5 percent; and "C" with less than 5 percent. All those ranked in the C category must reach the B category within one year.

6. To further encourage competition among the divisions, it is decreed that "if products are of good quality and lower cost, don't hesitate to buy from our competitors."

The accounting division (*keiri honbu*) monitors the financial health of each division. There are over 1,500 employees in this division. Unlike employees in other divisions, *keiri honbu* employees are not transferred to other divisions to perform other duties. They go through a training period of nine years and always remain accountants. The only exception to this principle of non-transfer is when they become assistants to heads of other divisions to handle those divisions' accounting work.

Kyocera's Ameba Unit

Kyocera extends the principle of independent accounting one step further. Its accounting unit is called an ameba unit, comprised of two to three workers, or twenty to thirty, depending on the project. In Kyocera, there are always about 400 such units in operation. Kyocera produces ceramic materials for the electronic industry, industrial ceramics, semiconductor parts, electronic components, electronic equipment, cameras and other consumer related products. As varied as its products are, manufacturing processes and materials needed also vary widely.

The income of an ameba unit is its sales, either to the outside or to another unit within the company. From the sales figure, all costs except personnel are deducted to obtain a "net sales" figure. Costs to be deducted include materials cost, work done by persons not in the ameba unit, repair cost, utility cost, amortization cost and the 10 percent margin to be paid to the marketing division. The "net sales" figure is then divided by the total hours worked by ameba unit members. This final result is posted on bulletin boards everywhere in the company.

Naturally there is a desire to do one better than the next team. To cut costs, as one of the ameba unit members commented, "We had better know something about man-hour reduction and quality control." Heads of ameba units are allowed to make contact with outside suppliers directly. It gives them a chance to know more about business practices and provides an excellent training ground. Incidentally, in selecting the head of a particular ameba unit, the seniority system is disregarded. The person who is the most energetic and suitable is selected, and often it is a woman. Some call it a challenge to Japan's vertical society but it is not inconsistent with QC's participatory principles.[9]

Pentel's Signal Control

The Matsushita and Kyocera systems encourage teamwork and promote intergroup competition by the use of independent accounting. The same goals are achieved by Pentel through its "signal control" system for observing and evaluating the performance of its separate divisions.

The signal control system applies the principle of visual control to corporate meetings. When various control charts are presented at a meeting, participants color code them according to the standards set for each project. Four colors — green, blue, yellow and red — are used by Pentel for this purpose. These colors represent the following:

Green — Going above the limit permitted by the management guideline. There is no serious problem, so it can be continued as is for now. If this signal continues for a period of three months, however, the person in charge of the project or division must analyze the cause or causes and establish countermeasures. Often this comes from the inability to establish a good plan or from unexpected occurrences.

Blue — Normal management practices are followed. Continue as before.

Yellow — Usually indicating abnormalities occurring suddenly. The method of operation may be at fault and countermeasures must be implemented within three months.

Red — The worst case possible. There must definitely be a persistent failure in the method of operation. Project teams centered around the division responsible must be organized to determine the cause or causes. In principle, countermeasures must be drafted and implemented within three months.

The control charts cover sixteen items from profits, sales and inventory to personnel. At the managers' meetings, the heads of those divisions with the largest number of red and yellow signals are placed in the "hot seat." While not intended for "inquisition," in a culture that shuns shame the hot seat serves as an effective deterrent against poor performance. Colleagues, however, are helpful when they discuss common problems, helping those in the "hot seat" with suggestions to prevent recurrence. The lesson is learned by all, not just by those singled out. Everything is done in the best tradition of QC by controlling the process and not the results.

SEVEN TOOLS OF TQC

Total quality control means exactly that. Everyone participates in quality control, from top executives down to line workers. Workers' participation is made easier by examples set by others and also by the fact that tools for QC implementation are easy to use.

When workers are first exposed to QC, they are often taught the elementary statistical method or the so-called seven tools. The texts are usually prepared locally using examples from the workplace. The seven tools are as follows:

1. *Pareto chart* — follows Pareto's principle of "vital few, trivial many."

2. *Cause-and-effect diagram* — shows the relationship between characteristics and cause factors. From its shape, it is nicknamed the fishbone diagram. It is also known as the Ishikawa diagram, after its inventor.

3. *Stratification* — grouping together data with common denominators to facilitate identification of problems.

4. *Check sheet.*

5. *Histogram* — gives graphic representation of a frequency distribution.

6. *Scatter diagram* — analyzes correlation through the determination of median; in some instances, binomial probability paper is used.

7. *Graph and control chart* — for example, the Shewhart control chart.

The seven tools are simple yet effective, solving as much as 95 percent of all problems. They are used by everyone, including top executives, engineers and line workers. The line workers' familiarity with the concepts of these tools gives them a common vocabulary they share with white-collar workers, which further facilitates their communication.

The fact that these seven elementary statistical methods are chosen specifically to become the seven tools is no accident. They are likened to the seven tools of Benkei, the legendary master warrior who lived in the twelfth century. The term "seven tools" is a household word, conveying the image of power, resourcefulness and easy accessibility. That is the way Japanese workers have been handling their QC activities.

These seven tools are tools for statistical quality control, and are especially effective where data can be quantified. But when data cannot be quantified, can QC remain valid? There is a movement afoot, centered around Osaka, to enter into a new area of non-quantitative analysis by creating seven new tools of QC. Within the rubric of QC, the seven new tools show how consensus can be reached in meetings, in marketing decisions, and so forth, by carefully studying the known to explore the unknown. The new seven tools are as follows:

1. Affinity chart

2. Correlation chart

3. Distribution diagram

4. Matrix chart

5. Matrix data analysis

6. Arrow diagram and program evaluation and review technique (PERT)

7. Process decision program chart (PDPC)

The new seven tools have proven effective in their application. For example, in analyzing its difficulty in providing lightweight steel sheet piles to Toyota under the latter's just-in-time system, Sumitomo Metal was able to identify problems such as its own relative inefficiency in production and the lengthy time taken in changing from one roll to another. At the same time, it could also point out Toyota's "frequent order changes," "erratic specifications with regard to size" and "inability to articulate its substitute quality characteristics" as causes for the difficulty. The seven tools were utilized to arrive at a solution satisfactory to both parties.[10]

A SENSE OF PARTICIPATION

When a line worker can use the seven tools of QC to suggest a change for the company, he is using the same language managers use and knows that he is part of the team. This sense of participation is pervasive in Japanese companies and the workers' enthusiasm for QC has an infectious quality to it. Mizutani Toshio, senior executive director of Pentel, worked day and night to get the Deming application prize, and when it was finally announced he cried. So did his secretary, and cry they did with those who were around them. At that moment they were all members of one big Pentel family.

Dedication to quality often transcends company boundaries. Mukai Yoichi, assistant manager of Toyoda Gosei's Haruhi plant, was asked to tape the conversations between his president Nemoto Masao and a foreign visitor. The tape of the morning session took beautifully but the afternoon sessions were not recorded. Mukai discovered that the batteries were low and while the tape moved, the batteries were not powerful enough to make a recording.

If this matter had been left as it was, it would not have been any different from any other taping miss. But Mukai did something different. He had a colleague check the tape recorder carefully to confirm his own observation. He wrote a QC lesson for the "one point QC" series, showing how recurrence could be prevented through testing. He sent his findings to Sony suggesting that (1) if batteries are low and unable to record, the tape must be made to stop; (2) an alarm be installed when the recording on one side of the tape is over; and (3) an indicator be provided on the button showing if the tape recorder is merely playing or recording.

When Mukai sent his "complaint" to Sony, "getting after Sony" was far from his mind. On the contrary, by checking a Sony product carefully, and pointing out its defects, he was doing Sony a favor. In Mukai's mind and in the minds of many others, businessmen are supposed to help one another and, when another's product does not perform well, to extend help in the form of providing the information needed by the manufacturer to correct defects. Sony's response came within a week.

Abnormality Control Chart

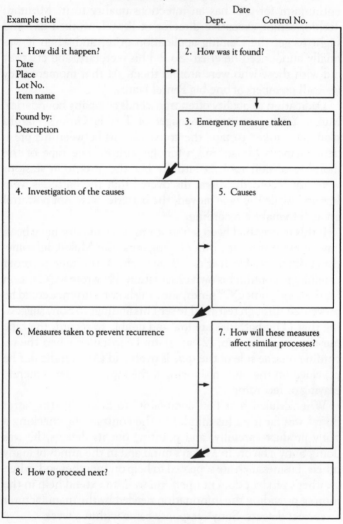

Date

Example title   Dept.   Control No.

1. How did it happen?
   Date
   Place
   Lot No.
   Item name

   Found by:
   Description

2. How was it found?

3. Emergency measure taken

4. Investigation of the causes

5. Causes

6. Measures taken to prevent recurrence

7. How will these measures affect similar processes?

8. How to proceed next?

Retain this summary sheet for future reference

QC's "market in" philosophy takes in customers as partners in the creation of quality products. "Customer complaint is a voice from heaven," says Honda Electronics of Toyohashi in its corporate philosophy. President Honda Keisuke's explanation is to the point: "When we receive complaints from our customers, they teach us something about our products. They save us a lot of performance tests and help us reduce our research and development cost. We always want to be close to our customers. It is because of them that we can be in business." With this, QC comes full circle and the control cycle is complete.

REFLECTIONS

To establish a good quality control program depends largely on the willingness of all workers concerned, especially those who are top managers.

The steps to be taken are not necessarily difficult but changes in attitudes are. It is for this reason that Dr. Ishikawa Kaoru speaks of QC as a thought revolution in management.

The following checklist is a short one primarily to let you reflect on the thought processes or attitudes that may or may not be conducive to a successful QC movement:

Is your company committed to quality first?
- If so, is it willing to forego an immediate profit statement in the quarterly report in favor of a long-range development plan?
- Is your company willing to invest in its "human resources"?

Is your company committed to the "market in" philosophy?
- Does your company take customer complaints seriously?
- When complaints are received, is there a mechanism that allows information to filter to design engineers, manufacturing engineers and line workers?

Do you take the opinions of your line workers seriously?
- Are you willing to let those working for you and those perhaps less educated than you show you a better way of doing things?
- Can your workers speak their minds without fear of retribution?

Do you encourage cross-fertilization of ideas between people in different divisions and between those who serve different functions?

Can your different divisions work under the slogan "The next process is our customer?"

Are you willing to look into your organizational structure and make necessary reforms even if it may not serve your own personal goals?

Are you willing to utilize another way of uncovering facts and data?

Can you view things from the perspective of others, especially those working under you and those who are your customers?

Do you know how many workers in line X are left-handed or ambidextrous?

You do not have to have answered "yes" to all of these questions to start a quality control program in your company. Even if you have had many negative answers, commend yourself for your own candor and honesty. QC needs honesty to succeed!

Finally, you may be wondering why a worker's left-handedness is made an issue in the checklist. At a major computer plant, it was discovered that many wiring mistakes had occurred because of the placement of the soldering iron uniformly to the right-hand side of the worker. Once these soldering irons were placed to the left-hand side for left-handed workers, many instances of wiring miss disappeared. This discovery was made by a QC circle that met informally to discuss better work procedures. As a manager you cannot always know what is needed. QC can help you discover it, as this example shows. When these steps taken by QC circles are combined, they become a fumble-free run for your company to reach its goal of quality assurance.

CHAPTER 6

The Art of Survival

There is a saying in Japan, *Kannan nanji o tamanisu*: Trials and tribulations are only meant to test one's mettle, and when they are over, one emerges as shiny as the most precious of jewels. In short, "Adversity makes a man wise." In the highly competitive Japanese business world, bankruptcy is no stranger. The market the company has been relying on may suddenly collapse and a massive recall may be ordered. No company is immune from the vagaries of the marketplace, and even the best known have faced extinction. These crises are like baptism by fire; well-managed companies emerge stronger and weaker ones perish. For the surviving company, the crisis forges a bond of unity among those who have shared the experience, making their commitment to the company and each other stronger.

SURVIVAL OF THE COMMUNITY-ORIENTED

Mazda in 1977-78

Mazda is a classic example of this threat-of-extinction and survival drama. Without the help of the community and Sumitomo Bank, it might not have survived.

In 1977-78, Mazda required a massive rescue attempt by a group headed by the Sumitomo Bank. Surrounding conditions were as follows:[1]

1. On November 10, 1978, the one millionth Wankel rotary engine-powered car Sabana RX7 rolled off the assembly line, eleven and a half years after its initial mass production. In spite of its power and other technological superiority, the engine was a mixed blessing for the company.

2. When this engine was installed the unit price of the car rose by about ¥ 100,000. In the initial stage of its development, rotary engine-powered cars broke down frequently without an adequate service network to repair them.

3. Mazda went ahead, along with Honda, in implementing the Muskie standards for environment protection with this rotary engine. This again increased the cost of the car while raising the level of its fuel consumption. Rotary engine-powered cars still showed some promise, but with the onset of the first oil crisis any advantage it might have had suddenly disappeared.

4. Meanwhile, Mazda neglected new car development.

5. Mazda had 121 dealer companies with a combined total of 1,301 outlets across the company. This figure ran fairly close to those of Toyota and Nissan with 1,937 and 1,540 respectively. However, each Toyota outlet sold an average of 538 cars annually and Nissan's, 507 cars. In contrast, Mazda lagged far behind, selling only 284 cars. Its peak year was 1962 when each outlet sold an average of 810 cars. Since then, it had gone down steadily by 10 percent each year.

6. Mazda seldom gave dealer incentives. Their margin was 13 to 14 percent as compared to the 18 percent other car dealers enjoyed. There was a great deal of animosity among the dealers against Mazda.

Sumitomo and Mazda

The exact loss sustained by Mazda in 1977 has never been

made public. It was estimated, however, to be several times the amount incurred by the Sumitomo Bank in the bankruptcy of Ataka, one of Japan's major trading companies. After writing off an amount of ¥ 113,239 million as bad debt for Ataka in 1977, Sumitomo was not ready to assume another loss. Bankruptcy for Mazda loomed large, and no other bank was willing to come around without the assistance of its main bank Sumitomo.

Mazda was then, as now, the largest employer in the prefecture of Hiroshima, which in 1977 had a population of 2,671,000. The city itself was ranked Japan's eleventh largest with a population of 844,000. If Mazda went, the entire regional economy would be seriously affected.

Help finally came from Sumitomo conditioned on a management shakeup that included the resignation of Matsuda Kohei, third president of the company. Matsuda, known for his autocratic style of leadership, was still highly respected by the community as the man carrying on the Matsuda family's tradition.

Negotiations to effect these changes involved the president of the Sumitomo Bank (Isoda Ichiro), presidents of two local banks (Ito Isao, president of the Bank of Hiroshima, and Morimoto Tooru, president of the Hiroshima Mutual Bank), two other local industrialists, and a cabinet minister (Miyazawa Kiichi, then Director of the Economic Planning Agency, and a member of the Diet from Hiroshima). The president of the Japan Chamber of Commerce, Nagano Shigeo, who happened to be from Hiroshima, served as the go-between.

It was not a happy day for Mazda on December 17, 1977 when Matsuda Kohei resigned, replaced by Yamazaki Yoshiki. A Sumitomo man was already serving as vice-president, and another appointed as director of the president's office. One director each was sent from the Sumitomo Bank and Sumitomo Trust and a third came from Sumitomo Trading Company. The management shakeup also involved a wholesale change of seven division general directors.

Henry Ford II came to Mazda and agreed to purchase 25 percent of its outstanding stock, opening the way for cooperation between the two companies. In this important move, Sumitomo also took the initiative.

While Sumitomo's actions were highhanded, reforms went smoothly. The majority of division managers and section chiefs were either transferred or retired, reducing the average age of middle managers from 45.5 to 43.4 in 1978. A division was no longer allowed to base its budget on the previous year's. Under the zero budget system, the next year's request would have to be properly justified, forcing each division to reevaluate priorities and establish a long-range plan.

There was to be no unilateral decree from the president's office. Conferences were to be held among company directors as often as necessary. Broad outlines of company policy were also to be approved by the directors. Meetings, however, were not to last longer than one hour. Delegation of power was institutionalized to facilitate prompt decision making.

Sumitomo's restructuring of Mazda reminds one of Ford's restructuring by the Whiz Kids in the post-Henry Ford, Sr. era. They were outsiders and finance men like many of the Whiz Kids. The animosity that developed between finance and car people at Ford did not materialize at Mazda, however. There, reforms spread to the workplace and dealerships. The Ford reforms kept the Whiz Kids in positions of power at the expense of traditional manufacturing people. At Mazda, it was a grassroots movement, not favoring any particular power groups.

"Customers First, Dealers Second and Makers Last"

With the posting of the slogan, "Return to the basics," reforms also began in the workplace. Workers were asked to question existing procedures and not remain blind to often overlooked problems. As the first step in rationalization, a movement was begun to reduce the amount of stored parts by half. This would require closer coordination between the processes and make the lines resemble Toyota's.

All types of waste became visible under rationalization and man-hour reduction was conducted in earnest. Those workers no longer needed were asked to go to the dealerships to get sales knowledge. It was a desperate move but the alternative would have been a massive layoff. It was at a time when poor sales forced the company to reduce its output by 5,000 cars. In January 1980, the first group of 1,100 workers left Hiroshima for various locations in Japan to begin their sales apprenticeship. By 1982, 5,000 workers were sent out in this euphemistically-called "sales expansion" movement.

These workers, turned salesmen, were to serve two years away from their families and the security of a regular paying job. To many it was torture to wear coat and tie. When customers did not come to the dealership, the worker-salesmen went door to door. In the city of Kasugai, a bedroom community for Nagoya and Toyota territory, one worker discovered that out of the forty-seven families he visited, only one had a Mazda car. It was a humiliating experience.

"We thought we were making good cars," or "We used to think whatever we made should be sold," they would write home. In an unsubtle way, workers and salesmen were being educated.

One positive effect of this movement, aside from teaching the workers that cars must be made to fit customers' needs, was a renewed appreciation of the difficulty encountered in making sales. As Mazda executives observed this, they realized that their previous attitude of "product out" was one of the factors bringing the company to the brink of disaster. Relationships with dealers improved, and a system of "customers first, dealers second and makers last" was developed. A sobering slogan, "Without sales there can be no production," was coined to remind executives and line workers alike of the importance of marketing.

Not everything went smoothly. Grumbling persisted among the workers. Rationalization came too quickly. "It's getting tougher and tougher to work every day, but where does it lead us?" was a common complaint. When the cycle time — the time allocated to complete a process — was set at fifty-five seconds, machines guided the worker's every movement. Foremen acquired greater responsibility without corresponding pay or authority. Considering it an intrusion, cooperating companies reluctantly accepted the offer of "honeybees" (QC specialists offering technical assistance). Yet, in spite of this, no one resisted rationalization. The crisis was too real and their self-survival instinct united them.

The local business community generously supported Mazda, which had been part of it since 1920. The Chamber of Commerce unofficially promoted a movement called "Buy Mazda." Four former presidents of the Chamber were asked to help form an organization called "A Committee to Promote Home Industries." It was a practical yet typically Japanese solution. Hiroshima's local economy could not sustain itself if Mazda faltered, so "Buy Mazda" was in part self-serving. But there was another reason. Local businessmen wanted to repay the Matsuda family for its three generations of support for Hiroshima and its civic endeavors. The business community resented the Sumitomo's intrusion in insisting that Matsuda Kohei be removed as president.

After recovery, the company was officially renamed Mazda (in Japanese, Matsuda) from its cumbersome former name of Toyo Kogyo K.K. While not promoted as such, it was a move to honor the Matsuda family. The $3 million price tag to effect the name change was no problem for a company that was finding renewed prosperity. In name and spirit, Mazda has come full circle and maintained continuity.

Unlike Chrysler's bailout, which involved the U.S. government and became an important political issue, the bailout of Mazda was done quietly without the Japanese government. It was true that Miyazawa Kiichi influenced some of Mazda's discussions. In that particular situation he was not acting as a cabinet minister, however, but as a "local boy" who made it big in Tokyo and wanted to help his home prefecture. There was no Loan Guarantee Board, only Sumitomo's good name as the main bank able to organize a consortium for Mazda's rescue.

Mazda did not have to issue stock warrants as Chrysler did, representing a potential dilution of its equity. The power Mazda surrendered was far less than Chrysler's in a comparable situation.

Mazda accepted directors sent from Sumitomo. In sending them, however, Sumitomo was merely following its standard procedure and had no intention of taking over management responsibilities from the company. The Sumitomo directors were there primarily to provide technical expertise and outsiders' perspectives for the benefit of the host company. A system was worked out to allow these directors to remain loyal to both Mazda and Sumitomo. For some, this would be the last assignment, with their career ending at Mazda. For others, it would be temporary with their return to Sumitomo contingent on their good performance at Mazda.

The Japanese system appears rigid but can be rather flexible. The interchange of managers as directors in this fashion helps both parties. When and if they return to Sumitomo, those directors would have acquired an appreciation of how a struggling company operates. There is cross-fertilization of management know-how both ways.[2]

In Sumitomo's decision to rescue Mazda, Ford played an important part. The latter's decision to invest in 25 percent of Mazda's stock could not have come at a better time. It lifted a big burden off Sumitomo as Mazda's main bank. Mazda's worth as a car company was fully reaffirmed through Ford's action. Yet in the end, the community's support proved decisive. It was a case of survival of the community-based.

Taio Paper

The community has also played a significant role in the survival of Taio Paper, Japan's fourth largest paper company with 6.2 percent of the market share. Established in 1943 under wartime regulations, it survived the postwar period of industry attrition to grow into a company with one of the most modern facilities.

It prospered through the 1950s, but when demands for paper fell in 1961, its fortune quickly turned. In 1962, it asked for protection under the company reorganization law, essentially a Chapter 11-type reorganization.

Several factors contributed to this sudden turn of events:

1. While the company possessed the newest machines, they were not properly installed and employees were not well trained to handle them.

2. The company did not have its own distribution system and relied on the traditional ones consisting of the manufacturer's dealers, wholesalers in prefectures, retailers and finally consumers. This distribution system was established by Oji Paper, whose prewar share of the market was close to 80 percent but recently only about 9.9 percent. Taio and other makers used this distribution system and sold their products well as long as demands were strong. When the market weakened, however, Taio's products were among the first cut from the distribution system.

The reorganization lasted over two years, ending finally in 1965. The crisis, however, created several positive results:

1. The community became more conscious of the company's importance. Taio was already the largest employer in the city of Iyo Mishima. Its employees came from the surrounding farming areas. They planted their cash crops and came to work in the factory. Farming alone could not sustain them and, if their factory jobs were lost, they would have to move elsewhere. Survival of the factory therefore affected farming in the area as well.

2. Aside from Taio, there were a number of small paper companies operating in the area who did not produce their own pulp. If Taio were to go bankrupt and cease operation, disruption in the supply system would have a serious ripple effect on these smaller companies.

3. As a result, a consensus was developed in the community to support Taio. Local financiers were willing to pay 20 percent above the face value of the reorganization bonds issued by Taio. Equally important to this show of support was the community's decision to pursue the creation of an industrial park on the Inland Sea through reclamation, allowing Taio a modest modern

plant there. In the 1970s, it became reality.

4. Since then, Taio has moved aggressively into automation and computerization, with the result that in many respects its plants resemble those of the most modern steel plants. Every process is automated — from energy control to turning chips into pulp. Like some steelworks, chips and other raw materials are brought to one side of the factory by ship, while finished rolls of paper exit by boat to different destinations from the other side, thereby eliminating the need for storage. The company's three plants and twenty-nine local sales offices are all connected by a computer network.

5. To support automation, intensified employee training is given. QC activities have also become a significant force within the company.

6. The company has aggressively created its own distribution network with over 400 salesmen going from one retail outlet to another, promoting various Taio paper products. The number of salesmen is close to twice that employed by Oji whose total sales are about 1.8 times that of Taio.

On November 1, 1982, Taio's stocks were again traded on the Osaka Stock Exchange, signifying its complete recovery. By then it was already the fourth largest paper manufacturer in Japan with the highest profit ratio in the industry. Its octogenarian president Ikawa Isekichi does not deny that his management style is not just "top down" but "super top down," leaving no doubt who is in charge. He explains, however, that the best management technique is one in which the owner of a small enterprise knows everything there is about the company. Even though Taio has become a company with 2,700 employees, the same principle applies.

While wandering around the plant, he and his managers are receptive to suggestions. The company's improvement groups (not called QC circles) come up with suggestions to save the company time and money, ranging from better maintenance practices to better telephone manners. "Our decisions are made top down, but suggestions for improvement have always been bottom up," says Toyoda Sadao, plant manager and company director. Participation is the key.

Taio is blessed with a group of dedicated workers. The company operates on three shifts, with employees divided into four groups. No one is on the same shift consistently. Changes in sleep patterns and daily routines create difficulty, but Taio employees are used to it and hardly grumble. Workers can rise in the wee hours of the night, harvest and assemble their cash crops, and deliver them to the vegetable market by five in the morning before coming to work for the first shift. It is a pattern of life everyone seems to accept.

Taio is the dominant presence in this city of 35,000 and its towering chimneys and ships carrying wood chips and paper rolls are constant reminders. Yet to call Iyo Mishima a mere company town is a misnomer. The company cannot exist without the city. Its citizens have demonstrated that through their purchase of Taio's reorganization bonds at a 20 percent higher premium, and their dedicated work for the company. The company is well aware of this and, in more than one sense, the city and Taio have become partners. Next to the city hall, across a narrow street, there is a smaller building housing the local chamber of commerce. The two buildings are joined by a bridge allowing city and chamber officials to transact their business informally. The bridge symbolizes the symbiotic relationship developing between the city and the business community.

Kadoma, Moriguchi and Toyoda

Kadoma and Moriguchi are not precisely household words, but they are the names of two cities to the east of Osaka, representing the headquarters of Matsushita and Sanyo, respectively. To enter Kadoma is to experience both the corporate philosophy of Matsushita and the personality of its founder, Matsushita Konosuke. In front of Matsushita's Central Laboratory, statues of eleven forerunners in modern sciences and technology are erected. They are Thomas Edison, whose statue occupies the honored central position, Anton Philips, Guglielmo Marconi, Georg Simon Ohm, Andre Marie Ampere and Michael Faraday. The Japanese contingent is represented by Toyoda Sakichi, founder of Toyota, and four from the Tokugawa period (1603-1867): Hiraga Gennai (1723-79), who first experimented with electricity in Japan; Sakuma Shozan (1811-64), said to have experimented with telecommunication before the coming of Commodore Perry; Hashimoto Sokichi (1763-1836), who through his study of Dutch books wrote the first book on electricity in Japanese; and Seki Takakazu, an eighteenth century Japanese mathematician whose theories of equations and determinants closely paralleled those in the West.

These statues were erected in 1968 to commemorate the centennial of the Meiji restoration and the fiftieth anniversary of the founding of Matsushita. In 1968, the Japanese people were still unsure of their acceptance into the academic world and of their own creativity. A large number of Japanese luminaries were represented because Matsushita wanted to suggest that the Japanese can be just as innovative as any Westerners. With the exception of Toyoda, all came from the period when Japan was closed to the outside world. One implication is that without Western assistance, Japan could develop her own technologies. Edison was still placed in the center, however, because like Edison, Matsushita had also had little formal education. Incidentally, the filament used in the first electric bulb came from a bamboo found near Kadoma. That made Edison's selection perfect because, after all, he needed Kadoma and so did electric bulbs.

Moriguchi is a city next to Kadoma and yet the two are quite different. Each hosts one of the most important electric appliance corporations, and they have always been rivals. Sanyo was founded by Matsushita's brother-in-law, Iue Toshio, who has seen to it that the company is not governed by any edifice complex. Sanyo has no fancy statues near its headquarters, but the town has its own ghost — that of the Konoike family. The Konoikes were the wealthiest family of the Tokugawa period but, after the coming of the Meiji restoration, it misjudged the changing times. Today the Konoike family is no more, leaving only a few place names behind.

Living in its shadows, Sanyo does not want to be left behind in the changing world. It stresses long-term forecasting and analysis of customer needs and legislative, political, macroeconomic and technological changes that may affect the company's future. It has not lagged behind any other electric and electronics makers in establishing overseas manufacturing plants. Knowing also that the Konoike and others failed by losing touch with the people, Sanyo insists that it is a people's company and avoids any semblance of elitism. It is down-to-earth and highly competitive. Appropriately its slogan is "catch up and move one step ahead." To reach this goal, it insists on "reducing cost by 10 percent on all products having the same quality as others, and increasing the 'merit' by 10 percent on products with the same price."

Toyoda is, of course, the city Toyota has made famous, and it is not necessary to say anything further than that it is located about eight miles east of Nagoya, and had it not been for Toyota, it might have remained a small farming village.

Thomas Peters and Robert Waterman said in their *In Search of Excellence* that well-managed companies usually do not have headquarters in major cities. This principle also holds true for Japanese companies. Matsushita, Sanyo and Toyota have several competitive advantages over their rivals. Their locations in Kadoma, Moriguchi and Toyoda mean that they can recruit line workers locally with similar values and experiences.

Just as American high school graduates can recall a certain football or basketball victory years after their graduation, a certain common experience binds these local people together. They speak the "same language" and have fewer discipline problems because of the watchful eyes of their neighbors and parents. They have looked up to the company as they have grown, and their entry into the ranks represents recognition of their coming of age. It is easier to train a group of people like this and create a strong and binding team spirit. Nissan, located near Tokyo, has had to recruit its workers far and wide. Its labor difficulties may be explained in part by the existence of many "rootless" workers in its midst. Toyota has been spared this.

Hiring locally is often extended to the management ranks. It is one of the surest antidotes to elitism. At Sanyo, a graduate of Osaka University may be regarded as one of the elite, but more often than not, he is from a local town and, despite his degree, remains one of the boys. Matsushita Konosuke's antielitism is well known. He once wrote a book suggesting that Tokyo University be disbanded.

To be close to one's own community is a great asset. Toyota, Mazda, Matsushita and Sanyo will continue to be formidable competitors in the world arena because of their strong community base.

SURVIVAL OF THE EMPLOYEE-ORIENTED

Under the headline "Japanese Are Suffering, Unemployment Rises in a Shifting Economy," the Wall Street Journal in a front page article on November 6, 1986, describes the day an official of Hitachi Zosen came to Innoshima to tell the city council that 1,000 of its 1,200 jobs in a local shipyard would have to be eliminated:

> The councilmen were silent. Several of them stared out the window at the jagged mountain peaks, the deep harbor and the big cranes of the shipyard. Then one councilman lost his temper and spent nearly 15 minutes berating Hitachi for a lack of "social responsibility." The Hitachi man replied that things had reached the point where "keeping the company running is our number one social responsibility."

Unemployment has indeed become a hot issue in Japan. What is unusual about this incident, is that a layoff of a mere 1,000 thousand positions can still cause a big stir, while similar events in the United States may go relatively unnoticed. In the Innoshima case, the fact that the company kept these employees for months and even years without having confirmed orders has gone unnoticed.

Japanese companies go to extreme lengths to preserve the so-called lifetime employment system, whether expressly stated or not. They may engage in "rotational" layoffs, as some steelmakers have done, to share the burden equally without laying off any specific individual, or they may transfer long-term employees to lesser positions with affiliates. A wholesale termination of employment is absolutely the last resort. It is seldom practiced and the criterion used is that of "social responsibility." In concrete terms, it simply means how well the company has taken into consideration the employee welfare.

In growth years, practicing lifetime employment poses no burden to the company. If anything, it is cost effective, because as the company fills the new employee quota in its lifetime employment track, it can realize savings in per employee cost. In declining years, when retrenchment becomes necessary, these valuable "human resources" suddenly become a financial burden. The task of a well-managed company is to anticipate retrenchment in the growing years and establish a personnel policy accordingly. Such a policy can succeed if it is employee- and not profit-oriented.

Kanebo

Kanebo has been an illustrious name in the annals of Japan's business history. Established in 1887 as a textile manufacturer, it grew along with Japan's industrialization. By 1896, it was already the most profitable company in Japan. In 1911, it slipped to second, but regained the first position in 1923 and again in 1933. Throughout this period, it was also known for its generous stock dividend policies. It became the fourth in industrial ranking in 1943, exceeded only by three defense related companies. In 1950, it was still number four.

There were signs of possible difficulties as its rival Toyo Rayon became number one; but company management was confident and expansive. During the first decade of Japan's postwar recovery, it was one of a few companies that regularly sent its employees overseas. Along with the prestige that the company name accorded, this practice served as a magnet to attract some of the best and brightest college graduates to Kanebo.

By 1960, though, signs pointed to a downswing. It was ranked twenty-first, and textiles had to yield their premier position to steel, automobiles and household appliances. The choice awaiting Kanebo was a painful one. It either had to reduce its output of textiles significantly to remain profitable, or increase it significantly to overwhelm its competitors, but at a cost injurious to the company. Pulling back was out of the question because it would have eventually meant reducing employment. Part of Kanebo's strength had always been its cadre of good managerial employees and skilled line workers. These human resources had to be utilized and their welfare taken into account. In the crisis atmosphere of 1961, the following two-tier policy decision emerged, allowing Kanebo to take the shape it has today:

First, Kanebo strengthened its own textile lines by broadening its operations to become the only company in the world to manufacture all seven basic textiles (silk, cotton, wool, nylon, polyester, acrylic and rayon). It was in part a concession to its proud tradition, but it also allowed the company to experiment and produce different blends of textiles, thus enhancing its own competitive position. As a corollary to this came high fashion with its higher added values.

Second, the company moved into the cosmetics field. Kanebo had a subsidiary chemical company and the basic technology already available. As far as management was concerned, high fashion and cosmetics were interrelated, and marketing information for one could be used by the other. It was an area in which the company was confident its employees could adapt readily.

Kanebo entered the cosmetics field in 1962 and set up fourteen distribution companies. The venture has been a success. Presently Kanebo commands about 17 percent of the total market share in cosmetics. While only about 50 percent of Shiseido's, it is five times that of the next competitor, Max Factor. Kanebo can also point out with pride that while Shiseido may be number one in cosmetics, it lacks the breadth Kanebo enjoys in allied fields.

Several factors have aided in Kanebo's successful "diversification" into the cosmetics field:

1. The timing was correct. In 1962 when Kanebo introduced its cosmetics line, Japan was about to enter its unprecedented postwar growth phase with high personal income that could be diverted to items once considered frills. A few years later the same strategy would not work, as seen in the fizzled attempt of Teijin, another textile giant, to introduce cosmetics at the time of the first oil crisis.

2. Kanebo's superb sales network has been another factor. There are now seventy-two distribution companies servicing Kanebo's retail outlets.

3. The holistic approach of merging fashion with cosmetics has attracted consumers.

4. Kanebo has always been a trusted brand name. In prewar days, Ginza and Kobe's Motomachi stores were graced with silk from Kanebo, creating an image of elegance.

5. A short learning curve exists for employees transferred from one division to another. Information and skills have been interchangeable.

With its success in cosmetics, Kanebo decided to enter other areas, including Chinese medicine. Venturing into the Chinese herb medicine field seemed strange for a company concerned with high fashion and cosmetics. Beauty required a healthy body, however, and in the early 1970s, health was supposed to come from nature. Kanebo entered the herb medicine field, just as Japan's opening to China created a craze for things Chinese. The timing was perfect.

Herb medicine was to meet cosmetics in a different manner. The herb gromwell produces a purple pigment in its roots that has been used traditionally as a dye. Mitsubishi Petrochemical spent years investigating the possibility of increasing the amount of pigment that could be extracted. When it finally succeeded in multiplying cells in the roots through cultivation, it brought the result to Kanebo. The latter used it to create the best-selling bio-lipstick first marketed in February 1984.

From its inception, the bio-lipstick was a sensational hit. Young office workers and housewives alike associated the term "bio" with "cosmetics." Its promotion by the advertising giant Dentsu and the singer Matsuda Seiko also paid off handsomely. The lipstick was recognized as one of the year's five best products by the Japan Economic Journal.

Receiving this prize in 1984 rekindled the spirit of togetherness among Kanebo's five groups — textiles, cosmetics, medicine, foods and living environment (housing and so forth). They are autonomous operating units, but when there is a need, ad hoc product development committees are established, drawing in people from the separate divisions. They also share technology, the value of which has been amply demonstrated by the creation of the bio-lipstick.

Kanebo has come a long way, and it would not have happened had the company neglected to take into account its employees' welfare and capabilities when restructuring was required in the 1960s.

Sanyo and Overseas Production

A similar concern underlies Sanyo's success in overseas expansion.

In determining whether Sanyo should establish an overseas

manufacturing company, management's first concern is its effect on employment conditions at home. With the value of the yen rising sharply, there is an incentive to outsource parts production to Taiwan, South Korea and other locations in the Pacific Rim. If 1986 is any indication, however, Sanyo will import only a few TV tubes from South Korea, and continue to produce as much as possible at home to maintain its current employment level. This will mean a decrease in profits of about 50 percent, but management will accept it. It has taken other measures, such as merging Tokyo Sanyo with the parent company, to trim down the number of administrative personnel. Trimming down line workers is a different matter, however.

In establishing overseas manufacturing facilities, heretofore Sanyo has been guided by a principle established by its second president, Iue Kaoru. It calls for one-third domestic consumption, one-third exports, and one-third overseas production.[3] In other words, no more than 33 percent of Sanyo's total revenue must originate from overseas production.

When overseas plants are established, transfer of technology inevitably occurs. So far, Sanyo has been able to retain its highest technology in Japan, transferring overseas technology that is lower but not necessarily obsolete. The latter helps overseas production to proceed without posing a direct challenge to Japan's domestic economy. At the same time, the transfer of technology has actually provided an incentive for Sanyo in Japan to seek even more up-to-date technology for itself. By retaining the latest technology at home, Sanyo is also in command of components that bring in the highest added values. As far as Sanyo is concerned, it has transferred technology without causing Japanese jobs to be lost to potential overseas competitors.

Sanyo's practice is therefore similar to what Toyota is doing in the NUMMI plant it operates jointly with GM. There, Toyota insists on importing engine and other essential parts from Japan in the production of the Chevrolet Nova. It thus effectively denies GM a chance to challenge it in small car production.

Not all the electric appliance makers follow the lead set by

Sanyo in limiting offshore production. There are smaller makers, such as Mitsumi Electric, that are expanding their
Taiwanese, South Korean and Malaysian operations, actively
purchasing parts from them. They also show relatively better
performance records. In the final analysis, the issue is one of
corporate responsibility and business ethics. Are corporations
their brother's keepers? Sanyo, Matsushita, Sony and Toyota
seem to answer in the affirmative by keeping their employees
employed.

The thinking represented by Sanyo poses a serious challenge
to its American competitors. Japanese firms are not likely to
share their latest technology with their American counterparts, as America did with them. To do so creates unwanted future competitors, as they experienced in reverse order. They are
willing to forego current profits in order to remain competitive
in the future. They do not want to become hollow corporations
that are nothing more than sales agents for foreign products.
Thus, they maintain their employment level, creating a sea of
stability in a turbulent world.

There is something inherently wrong when an RCA executive can announce straight-faced that it was able to produce a
TV as good and as inexpensively as Sony, without mentioning
that it was made by RCA in Taiwan. Such a TV might help
RCA's earning record for several quarters but it will not create
an additional job in Camden, New Jersey, or Silicon Valley,
California. The jobs lost today are not just today's jobs, but accumulated skills and technology for tomorrow.

Some American pundits are fond of saying that Japanese
managers are farsighted and trained to think in long-range
terms. Actually Japanese managers are just as fallible as Americans, but they have not forgotten the basics. Taught to look
back to the days when their company was founded, they visualize
a group of sweaty fellows working side by side with the founder.
Taught to look after the welfare of their employees in difficult
times, they cannot bear to see the agonized looks on employees'
faces when they hear their jobs have been terminated. The

company that takes into account the capabilities of its employees when reorganizing and diversifying is likely to select a more suitable path and avoid the mistake made by some American companies of reaching out for companies or areas they know nothing about. There are fewer self-serving financial deals by management; only heartless and selfish people can contemplate corporate raids and golden parachutes. Thus a management philosophy that is employee-based has an advantage over one that is not: a built-in focus on the long-range benefit to the company.

SURVIVAL OF THE CUSTOMER-ORIENTED

Being customer-oriented is another dimension that can make companies less vulnerable to crisis.

Sony — Fighting to Regain Its Market Share

Literally and figuratively, January 31, 1984, was the longest day for Sony. Its stockholders' meeting lasted thirteen hours and thirty minutes, a record for Japan. This came on the heels of its less than satisfactory performance in 1983. That year, Sony and its allies lost rather decisively to Matsushita and its allies in the VCR battle. Beta, whose market share was 81 percent in 1977, dropped to 25 percent in 1983 with the remaining market captured by VHS. Overall, Sony's overseas sales were lackluster, especially in the Middle East and Central and South America. Morita Akio, until now an industrial folk hero and creator of Sony's phenomenal, almost legendary growth, was attacked for his arrogance and mismanagement.

"They don't tell us anything about a new product until a day before its introduction," a major dealer bitterly criticized. "They are arrogant, thinking that their technology is so superior it can take care of everything. Don't they realize that technology is leveling off and other manufacturers can catch up very quickly? If they would give us information earlier, we could provide them with the views of the customers."[4] The mighty Sony had fumbled because it forgot to survey the field and remember its customers.

The road to recovery was a tortuous one. Sony's typical response was another "Sony first" — the Walkman. A success in its initial introduction, it was soon beset by imitators — imitators with recording functions Sony's Walkman lacked. Sony led the compact disc field in 1982, but when Nippon Gakki produced a CD with a price tag of ¥100,000, Sony's dominance quickly evaporated. By the end of 1984, however, Sony fought back with a CD priced at ¥50,000. The lesson from the marketplace had finally been learned.

Amita's Net

If a major corporation cannot escape customer scrutiny, smaller companies are even more vulnerable. They have one advantage, however, over mightier and wealthier rivals — they cannot afford the luxury of being arrogant. With their ears firmly fixed to the ground, they are attuned to customer needs, sometimes uncovering their latent demands. Identifying such opportunities, they can move decisively. Amita, maker of the fishnet machine, is a case in point.

Amita's president, Yamamoto Tadashi, saw his first fishnet-making machine in 1915 when he was only six years old. His uncle brought back one from France but did not know how to use it. Before long, however, his uncle's shop was making rudimentary machines.

When Yamamoto first visited the United States, in 1952, none of the net machine manufacturers allowed him inside their factories. Observing some of the fishing nets in use, however, he judged that the Amita machines were just as good — if not better than those currently used in the United States. He decided to start exporting his machines overseas.

He had no sales organization, however. He searched through trade catalogues to identify potential customers, patiently wrote to them and always remembered to enclose a sample strand made by his machine. He attended trade fairs religiously and exhibited Amita machines whenever there was an opportunity. In 1957, an international fishing equipment conference in Hamburg gave Amita's machines a favorable mention. Finally orders started to come in from different parts of the world.

Without knowing it at the time, Yamamoto had devised a winning formula for custom-making machines to fit the needs of customers. Fishing needs vary from country to country. For trawl fishing the net must have large twines. The throw nets used in developing countries require only fine twines. Amita's machines are designed from the outset to produce different types of nets according to specification. They can both manufacture fishing nets and prepare twines for them. Its equipment can also knit, stretch and dye nets to specification. Both single and double knot knittings are available using monofilament and multifilament twines. The machines can also be downsized or expanded. With such flexibility, Amita's machines can meet the demands of different markets at any time. This flexibility also extends to parts and services. If a machine breaks down, even if it was purchased thirty-five years ago, Amita can still produce whatever parts are needed.

Amita sells directly to its end users, never relying on Japan's famed trading companies. Most of the end users in fishing villages are away from population centers, located where trading company men do not usually go. Sales are made by Amita's own employees who move from country to country, and from one fishing village to another. In fact any one who applies to Amita for a job is told to be prepared to spend three months overseas if married and a year if not married, engaged in sales activities. This requirement applies equally to engineers and line workers. There are seventy-one employees in all and most have had some foreign experience, an unusual accomplishment by any standard. In addition to domestic sales, its machines now reach sixty-two countries.

Once overseas, employees are encouraged to go native, so to speak, and forget Japanese. If there is a foreign airline service available, they are not to use Japan Airlines. They are asked to speak to local people as frequently as possible in their own language. An American employee named David Staples is married to a Japanese woman and speaks excellent Japanese. In the office, however, no one is permitted to speak to Staples in Japanese. At every opportunity, employees are encouraged to acquire skills in another language.

Ito Susumu is a veteran employee who has been with the company for thirty years. He has traveled to over sixty countries selling Amita machines. When Colonel Nasser was still governing Egypt, Ito became acquainted with him. The Egyptian diet normally did not include fish, but Ito persuaded Nasser to feed it to his soldiers. Ito then taught some of these soldiers how to catch fish. Gradually fishing became an important industry as the soldiers' eating habit spread to the general population. Expansion in the fishing industry created the need for fishnets and then for the net making machines. Of course Amita made its sale.

Ito still has in his possession a letter of appreciation from Nasser. He is commended for selflessly teaching the Egyptian people the art of fishing and for contributing to the expansion of Egypt's national economy. In this endeavor, Ito received some assistance from the trading company, Marubeni, but in most instances, Amita's work has always been done independently.

There is always something that will escape the "net" of large manufacturers and large trading companies. The Amita fishing net machine is a case in point, its success directly attributable to its closeness to its customers.

Kabushiki Shimbun and the Stock Market

The year 1986 saw the creation of a worldwide financial market, with the stock exchanges of New York, Tokyo and London brought together in close trading collaboration. Traders who work on the exchange floors, either in Tokyo, Osaka, Nagoya or in other cities, require up-to-date information. That is provided by the *Kabushiki Shimbun*, a specialized newspaper published on weekdays about the stock, bond and financial markets.

The *Kabushiki Shimbun* is only twelve pages and unpretentious in appearance. It costs ¥110 as against ¥80 for the *Nihon Keizai Shimbun* and other major Japanese newspapers. The *Nihon Keizai Shimbun* is Japan's counterpart to the Wall Street Journal, with excellent coverage of economics news. One would then expect the *Nihon Keizai* to be the paper for all the traders. The *Kabushiki Shimbun*, however, has carved a definite place for itself with a format and contents reflecting the needs of its customers.

An average Japanese trader commutes ninety minutes each way from his home to Kabutocho where the Tokyo Stock Exchange is located. Unlike other papers, the twelve-page *Kabushiki Shimbun* can be completed during the commuting time. The information contained is adequate and never excessive. The first two pages contain news on major developments. The next six pages are devoted to stock prices from the Tokyo, Osaka and Nagoya exchanges; local trading at cities like Kyoto, Hiroshima, Fukuoka, Niigata and Sapporo; over the counter markets; lists of most actively traded stocks; and most active stocks traded by foreigners. The last is included because Japanese exchanges tend to be influenced disproportionately by active trading from foreign sources.

The remaining four pages constitute the "money" section, summarizing the news from all over the world along with a special column in English. Aside from its listing of the domestic bond market, it also lists Euro international bonds, including Swiss Franc bonds and Deutsches Mark bonds, Euro Yen bonds and Samurai bonds. There are separate listings for the activities of the Federal Reserve Board, foreign governments bonds, foreign bond yields, foreign exchange rates, Euro money market rates and foreign call market rates. This money section is the brainchild of Kodama Koichi, the company president, and his young editorial staff, many of whom are in their twenties. Each of the listings in both sections are always published in the same corner of the same page each day, making it easier for busy traders to flip through to find the required information. In fact, each company's name appears on the same spot day after day so that once a person becomes used to the paper, he can open to the page and immediately find what he needs. The readership is not confined to traders. Its convenient format has made it a useful reference tool in all corporate offices.

Kabushiki Shimbun also maintains an information service center as a subsidiary. The service center provides information on the opening, high, low and closing price of any stock traded on the three major exchanges, and provides twenty-two charts, including a psychological line, to allow any stock trader to pass judgment on any stock at a moment's notice. The data bank is in the Tokyo home office, but any subscriber to the service can reach it through software provided by the company called SPIC-ACE and a NEC PC-980 personal computer. The company has a contract with NTT (Nippon Telephone and Telegraph) to feed its data to NTT's Demonstration Subcenters. Thus for most subscribers, the cost of inquiry is the subscription cost plus a local telephone call.

With this service, Kabushiki Shimbun is in the forefront, providing information for Japan's liberalized financial market. One may ask why this type of service has not been undertaken by a giant like the Nihon Keizai Shimbun. The simple fact is that Kabushiki Shimbun started much earlier, accumulated an impressive data bank, and in a sense cornered the market. It invested heavily in computers, an alternate source of power to protect the data bank, and personnel to collect and manage the data when such a venture was considered risky. Today's success is a payoff for the forward-looking planning completed six or seven years earlier. When asked about the secret of his success, Kodama responded modestly: "We have to thank our customers. They are the ones who told us we should start this type of service. All I had to do was find capable young men to provide the technical expertise, and we worked together as a team, with ideas often coming from customers and old hands in the company." That is good fumble-free management.

REFLECTIONS

Instead of our usual checklist, here are some questions to share with your colleagues and those who work for you. Ask them to respond, and use some of the representative responses as topics for discussion at your next QC circle meeting:

In my position in our company, what can I do to make our company more responsive to the needs of our community?

Do I really know the needs of our employees? Do I always simplify them in monetary terms?

In my present position in the company, what can I do to make our company become more aware of employees' needs?

In my position in the company, do I really listen to the voices of our customers?

Who are my customers?

In order of importance, as seen from my present position within the company, I would rank the following, with (1) being the most important:
· Those who are above me, especially my boss.
· Those who work for me.
· All other employees.
· Our customers.
· Our suppliers.
· Our community at large.

After completing the above, please write, in no more than five lines, your reasons for selecting a certain category as (1).

CHAPTER 7

American Companies in Japan

Whenever his country is criticized by Americans for the closed nature of its business practices, Prime Minister Nakasone is fond of saying that one only has to look at the examples of IBM, Coca Cola and McDonald's. Indeed these three companies have come to symbolize the American presence in Japan. Of the three, McDonald's is in the service-distribution sector where Japan is relatively underdeveloped, and neither the government nor the business community resisted its entry. The success stories of McDonald's and Kentucky Fried Chicken in Japan make fascinating reading. Statues of Colonel Sanders can be found everywhere and McDonald's Ginza franchise sells more hamburgers then any other store in the world. As the fast food industry is not treated elsewhere in this book, however, its inclusion at this stage will not serve any purpose.

Coca Cola manufactures and distributes soft drinks and has the distinction of having the majority share of this market. How it achieved this in a country that does not concede market shares to foreign concerns is worthy of discussion. The main focus of this chapter, however, will be devoted to IBM Japan, whose name was synonymous with the computer industry in Japan for many years before its dominance was challenged by the concerted efforts of the government and a group of Japanese companies. That it still remains a dominant force in Japan speaks well of its tenacity, corporate philosophy and management.

IBM JAPAN

IBM Japan has reached this plateau because it has always practiced Japanese-style fumble-free management. It is community-, customer- and employee-oriented. Word for word, its seven management principles are almost identical to those promoted in the best Japanese companies: "respect for the individual, finest service for our customers, pursuit of perfection, excellent management, responsibility toward stockholders, fair dealing in purchasing and contributing to society." IBM Japan has succeeded in Japan because its corporate culture is similar to those in Japan. There has been no painful transfer of an alien corporate culture to an inhospitable land.

Back in 1940, Gil Burck wrote for *Fortune* that at IBM "everyone addresses every man as 'Mr.' Company publications never refer to any man without prefixing a 'Mr.' to his name."[1] He was impressed by the company's concern not to make a sharp contrast between blue- and white-collar workers, its efforts to fill new jobs from within and its stress on teamwork. These same practices are keys to IBM Japan's success and are also deeply ingrained features of lifetime employment in Japan.[2]

Implementing the principle of "respect for the individual" calls for a system that insures that no one is lost in the organization and victim to unfair treatment. A formalized "speak-up program" insures anonymity to employees who wish to question, express opinions or even dissatisfaction to the top management. Under this program, communication is handled by the speak-up coordinator who responds to the employee initiating the inquiry within ten days. Once a response is given, the file identifying the sender in the coordinator's office is destroyed. When differences or dissatisfactions cannot be resolved through this program, an employee may seek an interview directly with the president under the company's "open door" policy, again with assurance of confidentiality. The company is so serious about this policy that it is fully explained to new employees during their initial orientation.

American managers' reaction to this type of program may be one of uneasiness if not horror. They may worry about the diminution in their authority or destruction of the chain of command. These programs have not been abused in IBM Japan, however. In a hierarchical society, employees respect those above them and do not resort to these programs unless absolutely necessary. It is true that these programs tend to moderate the behavior of managers, but not to the extent that they become over-solicitous of the feelings of their subordinates. There is rather a heightened sense of proper balance and a desire to be fair. Company president Shiina Takeo wanders around his plants and participates in QC circle activities. The approachability of top executives — a key ingredient in good Japanese management — is scrupulously maintained at IBM Japan.

Like other well-managed Japanese companies, IBM Japan uses rotation as a means of cross-fertilization of ideas and employee education toward advancement. When a new project team is formed, its personnel may come from as many divisions or sections as there are people, but no additional bureaucratic entity is formed. For example, when the Customer Satisfaction Program was formed to promote quality control, its personnel came from different divisions within the company. They served for different lengths of time in this new division before being transferred to other divisions. On a staggered timetable, new staff members were trained in quality control and transferred, becoming effective QC teachers in their own right. In the meantime, the Customer Satisfaction Program Division continued to report to Naruse Makio, one of the managing directors. Naruse's role, in effect, was to maintain the program continuity while division heads changed periodically.

Employees are selected for rotation through a search of computer files available on each employee. If there is not a suitable person available for a certain position, outside hiring is also considered. In this, IBM Japan departs from normal Japanese practices.

Employee education is intense. It consists of small group meetings, weekend seminars and seminars of longer duration, as well as sending employees to domestic universities and overseas. Time spent in these "reorientation" programs ranges from one week to twenty days for most workers. As managers climb the corporate ladder, more emphasis is placed on their managerial responsibilities, especially the personnel development area. At IBM Japan, those who have received reorientation in turn may teach the same subject to others. Teaching is the best way to learn and reinforce ideas.

As part of employee education, correct manners are drilled into the employee's consciousness. Its marketing personnel handbook, for example, speaks of what to carry on one's person, how to address others and how to answer an incoming phone call. It also suggests what to send and not send when there is a death in the customer's family. The same handbook asks IBM employees to be circumspect in public places. No one wearing an IBM badge, for example, is allowed to read a trashy magazine on a commuter train.[3]

There is a conscious effort by the company to manifest "Japaneseness" as part of its corporate behavior. A customer may tour IBM's domestic rivals, such as Fujitsu and NEC, for a computer. At these companies he hears computer jargon in English. At IBM, he finds these English terms carefully translated into Japanese for him. At the plants in Fujisawa and Yasu, some American computer manuals are translated into Japanese before workers start constructing a mainframe computer. Most of the engineers are trained bilingually and, at first sight, the translation may appear unnecessary. It actually serves several purposes, however. In the process of translation, some unclear passages may be made perfectly understandable, and using the Japanese manual in the construction of the computer may eliminate some manufacturing mistakes. In this, employee training, customer service and manufacturing integrity are combined in the act of translation.

The company's effort to be identified with Japanese culture has been continuous. IBM Japan actively supported a number of local Noh theaters, the oldest continuous theatrical form, which has not always found favor with modern young Japanese. It was an important cultural event when famed Kabuki actor Ichikawa Danjuro officially assumed his inherited theater name in April 1985. IBM Japan co-sponsored the event, donating a painting of "Two Birds with Auspicious Omens" by Kamimura Atsushi. A silk brocaded replica of the picture in the fashion of Nishijin was then given to select customers and friends.

A few years back, when *kanji* script first became available for word processing, IBM Japan used a Hiroshige woodblock print in its advertising campaign, to impress upon the public how good its resolution was. The company's cultural awareness, combined with its other image of a leader in modern technology, as shown in the Tsukuba science and technology fair of 1985, creates an irresistible corporate persona. What the Japanese seek themselves — knowledge of an elegant past and an understanding of the most modern — IBM as a company seems to possess abundantly.

While identifying closely with Japanese culture, IBM has deviated somewhat from the employment practices of other Japanese companies. Overtime is never forced on employees. If anything, employees are encouraged to leave work at a reasonable hour to be with the family or engage in cultural pursuits of their own. Employees are not asked to go through the round of after-hours parties. These practices, of course, are sacrosanct in other companies where no employee dares criticize them. American writers also tend to see only the positive aspects to these time-honored practices. At IBM, however, employees are free to criticize them. When asked why he chose IBM over Fujitsu, IBM's main competitor, one recent graduate engineer suggested without hesitation that he loved the freedom IBM provided. IBM has been able to attract some of the best minds in Japan from its best universities. Its "Americanness" in some personnel practices has been one of its drawing cards.

IBM headquarters at Roppongi is not as ornate as some others. President Shiina's office is functional and the framed computer chips presented to him for twenty-five continuous years of service tell the story. There are no oak double doors, plush leather or Louis XV antique chairs. The entire Roppongi headquarters, in fact, resembles an office without walls. Partitions can be removed and reorganized as assignments change. Voices heard in Roppongi are louder and more audible, occasionally sprinkled with laughter. That is one Americanism Japanese companies ought to learn from IBM Japan.

Time as an Ally

IBM has an advantage over other American companies in that it has been in Japan longer than most. In 1925, the first IBM machine was imported to Japan with the Morimura Brothers serving as the company's agent. The Japan Watson Adding Machine Company was established in 1937. Its assets were confiscated as enemy property during World War II, but were ordered returned in August 1949 by General MacArthur's headquarters. Its accumulated rental fees were also returned and, with these returned assets, International Business Machines Co. of Japan, Ltd. was formed. At that time there were sixty-six employees, consisting mostly of former Watson employees.

The company enjoyed an upswing in fortune during the Korean war, but the scope of its activities remained modest. In 1953, fresh from Bucknell University in Pennsylvania with an engineering degree in addition to his degree from Keio University, Shiina Takeo joined the company. Recalling these earlier days, the future president of IBM Japan cannot forget that the company's modest two-story head office in Kojimachi had a chicken coop next door. There were 200 employees then and everyone worked hard.[4]

IBM's machines, using the punch card system (IBM 602, 405), gradually found acceptance in the 1950s. Banks and insurance companies were impressed by the ability of the American occupation authorities' (GHQ) data processing and knew the secret was in the punch card system (PCS). As a means of promoting economic recovery, the Japanese government allowed importation of PCS tax free, and Nissan, Nippon Kokan, Mitsubishi Electric, Hitachi and the Japan Weather Bureau became its first users. IBM's main rival had been Remington, which in prewar years had 80 percent of the market share for its calculators. Luck was with IBM, however. Remington's distributor, Mitsui Trading was still suffering from the effect of the *zaibatsu*[5] dissolution ordered by the GHQ. Without a distributor in Japan, Remington had to yield the market to IBM.

The year 1958 marked the beginning of the computer age for Japanese industries. The first truly modern computer, the IBM 650, was installed at Tokaimura, Japan's nuclear research institute. Sanwa Bank became the second organization to import the same machine, and others followed. The corporate philosophy of service to customers was scrupulously followed. Professor Nozawa Reikichi of Tokyo Institute of Technology recalls his days as a research scientist at Tokaimura. "We could not figure out one specific problem, and indicated that to the company. A couple of days later when we finally figured out how to do it, we informed the company. We were told that engineers for the IBM 650 had already left Hawaii for Tokyo."

Organizationally, changes were taking place as the company began to grow. Consistent with IBM's policy of letting the host country's nationals manage its company, C. M. Decker, who headed the company since its inception in 1949, retired in 1956 to pave the way for the appointment of Mizushina Hiroshi as president. In 1959, the company's present name, IBM Japan, was adopted.

The 1964 Tokyo Olympics gave the public a foretaste of the power of computers. When over 5,000 athletes started competing in twenty different categories, the computer had to input each athlete's nationality, sex, weight. It also had to be programmed to know the rules of each separate event. At the closing ceremony, IBM Japan was able to hand to Avery Brundage, president of Comite Internationale Olympique, complete records of the fourteen-day event, a task that took the previous Rome Olympics two years to compile. According to one story, prior to the opening day a reporter was sent to cover preparations for the Olympics. He came upon a crate imprinted with IBM's logo. "To whom does this belong?" the reporter demanded. "It's IBM's," came the answer. "Don't you understand my question? Which company makes this thing you call IBM?" By the time the Olympics were ended, no one questioned who IBM was.

IBM Japan volunteered for the Olympics assignment, but its business payoff was almost instantaneous. Mitsui Bank's president saw how records were kept at the Olympics and ordered the same computer installed in his bank to initiate the Online Realtime System. It created a unified system of accounting for its forty-three branches within Tokyo. Other industrial applications soon followed. Kimitsu Steelworks produced 9.6 million tons of crude steel annually with 7,339 employees. Yawata Steelworks produced 9 million tons with 22,567 employees. Per capita, Kimitsu, using the IBM system, produced 1,308 tons against Yawata's 398 tons. Yawata soon followed suit by adopting the IBM production control system. NHK, with 640 television programs and 1,200 AM/FM radio programs each week, sought to create a support system. IBM Japan arranged for the IBM Federal Systems to develop it. Toyo Kogyo — now Mazda — began using IBM in its marketing operations, connecting its dealers directly with the company. In the days before the first oil crisis, Japan's GNP grew double digit annually, and IBM Japan grew with it.

The year 1971 was particularly good. The Yasu plant was completed, complementing the work of the Fujisawa plant finished four years earlier. The new headquarters building in Roppongi was completed, placing IBM close to Kasumigaseki and Nagatacho, where Japanese government offices are located. The Fujisawa Research Laboratories began its operations. The automated Nikkei newspaper editing and composing system became operational at the *Nihon Keizai Shimbun* (Japan Economic Journal). Under this system, reporters still wrote their articles and had the desk approve and edit them. They were input in the computer the way they were written in Japanese; however, the column length and entire page layout were all done by computer. The system is not too different from what present-day personal computers do, but it was a revolutionary concept anticipating the use of *kanji* (Chinese characters) in computers.

Challenge to IBM

The challenge to IBM Japan's dominant position came unobtrusively at first. There was a move toward "liberalization" of the computer market, which IBM fully supported. Had it been implemented at the beginning of the 1970s, IBM Japan would have been its beneficiary inasmuch as there was no viable competitor in sight worldwide. It would have been able to continue its role as the conduit in introducing computer technology to Japanese industry while making use of its U.S. connection and its own advanced technologies. IBM Japan was a U.S. subsidiary and a domestic manufacturer of computers since 1963, requiring no Japanese protection. Japanese politicians thought differently, however. No matter how many Japanese worked for IBM, it remained a foreign company. Their first obligation was to companies whose computer technologies were still in an early stage of development.

When computer companies resisted the move toward liberalization, Japanese politicians were able to delay it — partial as it was — until April 1976. In the meantime, in March 1971 the Japanese Diet enacted the Special Industries Law for the Electronics and Machinery Industries for "developing technology and reorganization." To prepare for liberalization, computer companies were offered ¥36 billion in subsidies in fiscal year 1972 with additional sums to be added in future years, provided they cooperated in research and production. This law resulted in the joining of Fujitsu with Hitachi and Mitsubishi with Oki to produce IBM-compatible computers, and NEC with Toshiba on noncompatible models.[6]

In 1976, on the day partial liberalization finally came, IBM Japan was probably five or six years ahead of these combined Japanese companies, technologically. Japanese companies cultivated their own technologies resourcefully, however, and had a clear focus for their common research. What they could not develop their own they borrowed from the United States wherever they could. Fujitsu, which parted company with Hitachi to develop its own computers, purchased a majority share in Amdahl, a prominent IBM compatible maker, as a means of learning IBM technologies.

In 1979, there was a serious shortage of memory chips in the United States. The Japanese, with the economies of scale acquired through their joint efforts, were ready to supply them. Afterwards, they maintained their newly gained market share and never yielded their position to U.S. companies seeking a comeback. With the new decade, Japanese companies were ready to challenge IBM at home in the United States and in Japan. It was the last frontier. After a series of victories, first in textiles, then in steel and television sets, and finally in automobiles, this was the last bastion of the U.S. industrial supremacy. The so-called three families — likening them to the three major daimyo families of the Tokugawa period — Fujitsu, Hitachi and NEC were ready, as were their main banks. It was true that their software was still behind in technology, but like the *zaibatsu* organization of yesteryear, they could spin off many small software firms vertically integrated with them.

The Industrial Spy Incident — June 22, 1982

On June 22, 1982, the FBI announced that several Japanese engineers and employees of Hitachi and Mitsubishi were arrested for attempting to steal secrets from IBM. They bought information concerning memory subsystems, and some of the engineers actually entered the plant floor and took pictures of the IBM 3081K, the new system expected to be announced the following year. At first the Japanese public received this news with indignation, calling the entrapment totally unjustifiable. There were demonstrations against IBM in front of its Roppongi headquarters. It was a no-win situation for IBM Japan. It could not openly support the stand taken by IBM's home office. To do so would be tantamount to declaring that IBM Japan had never been a Japanese company, an image it had cultivated for so long — nor could it repudiate its parent company. There was a principle involved. At the same time, the company could neither condemn nor condone the actions of Hitachi and Mitsubishi. They were IBM Japan's competitors as well as trading partners. What happened in California without its knowledge, if mishandled, could seriously damage IBM Japan's standing in Japan.

Shiina chose a typical Japanese solution. He called the presidents of Hitachi and Mitsubishi, explaining that he personally and IBM Japan had no advance knowledge of the event and expressed the hope that they could remain friends and trade as before. When your opponent is down, you do not trample him but show compassion. That is called *nasake*, and Shiina exercised it in this instance. Subsequently Hitachi and Mitsubishi pleaded no contest and paid a nominal sum in fines. In the ensuing civil suits and out-of-court settlement, however, Hitachi gave IBM rights to inspect and/or purchase Hitachi computers before they were sold, and agreed to pay an unspecified amount for damages. Fujitsu, which was not a party to the industrial spy incident, also entered into an agreement to respect IBM's copyrighted software materials and paid for its past infringement. The industrial spy incident strengthened IBM's overall competitive position vis-à-vis makers of its compatibles and reaffirmed its claim of superiority in computer software.

The Japanese public's perception — popularized by the press — is that IBM Japan had lost its dominant position in the computer industry by the early 1980s and the industrial spy incident was its desperate move to regain the lead. To support this conspiracy theory, they cite the fact that as of June 30, 1982, a week after the spy incident, of the computers in operation, those made by Fujitsu had a 27.7 percent share, far outdistancing IBM's 11 percent. The NEC/Toshiba group had 20.2 percent followed by Hitachi's 16 percent.

These figures are misleading, however, because they compare apples and oranges. In these statistics, the large mainframe IBM computers used at places like New Japan Steel are not differentiated from small rival computers used in downtown shops. Profits, which are more accurate in representing relative worth, indicate that for the same period, IBM Japan was first with 27.7 percent, followed by Fujitsu's 21.4 percent and Hitachi's 16.6 percent. IBM Japan has been resilient in this regard. In FY 1985, it had a pre-tax profit of ¥ 134,742 million. Fujitsu's pre-tax profit for the fiscal year ending March, 1986 was ¥ 57,685 million. In the year in question, IBM had 16,775 employees while Fujitsu had 48,383 employees. Per capita, the pre-tax profit was therefore ¥ 8.03 million for IBM and ¥ 1.19 million for Fujitsu. Granting that it was a particularly bad year for Fujitsu, if one substitutes the previous year's pre-tax profit of ¥ 126,782 million for this comparison, per capita would still come to only ¥ 2.62 million, or about 33 percent of that of IBM Japan.

IBM World's Role

In 1984, a new operating unit was formed in IBM's World Trade Corporation, named the Asia/Pacific Group. Its headquarters was established in Tokyo initially with about 200 employees. It was part of IBM/WTC's comprehensive reorganization attempt to delegate more power to its operating units. As far as Japan was concerned, however, the timing was not necessarily the best.

It was announced at a time when IBM Japan was successfully conducting a campaign as a "Japanese" corporation. Establishing the new operating unit headquarters right next to Hotel Okura and the U.S. Embassy had the opposite effect, however. Coming so soon after the industrial spy incident, the majority of Japan's press interpreted this move to be IBM's counterattack against the dominant role the Japanese computer industry had assumed in recent years. IBM — not just IBM Japan — was under close press scrutiny. Some reporters discovered that while IBM subsidiaries in West Germany, France, Great Britain and Italy were each given the status of an independent operating unit, Japan IBM was not. Speculation went wild. "Could it be that IBM no longer trusts IBM Japan's ability to compete because it has shamed IBM by yielding the top position to Fujitsu?" was a typical approach. They would then go on to show how Japan's computer industry had excelled.

Credit for not making this event a public relations disaster goes to George H. Conrades, Shiina Takeo and the employees they represented. Conrades was forty-five years old when he was appointed group executive to head the Asia/Pacific group. He had distinguished himself as vice president of the national marketing division, president of the national accounts division, and assistant group executive of information systems/technology group. He was an executive assistant to Frank Cary when the latter was chairman.

Well versed in IBM's inner workings, Conrades perceives his job to be one of bridge-building, to join Tokyo with Armonk, Beijing, Taiwan, Hong Kong and the rest of Southeast Asia, New Zealand and Australia. IBM Japan is made part of the group because its presence is needed to assist in the expansion of activities such as information networking. The seventeen nations served by the Asia Pacific group have more than half the world's population, and IBM Japan will play a dominant role. To Conrades, there is no diminution in the importance of IBM Japan to the parent company. If anything, its position has been enhanced.

Shiina finds the arrangement good for IBM Japan. Alluding to the press criticism of IBM's counterattack, he remarked, "It's nice having staff headquarters established in the fields to assist us." Many decisions previously requiring Armonk's consent can now be handled in Tokyo. Having someone of Conrades' stature, IBM Japan's needs are effectively and efficiently transmitted to the home office.

Conrades has learned Japanese customs quickly. "The Japanese people respect age, and Tak Shiina is ten or more years older than I. They know through my actions that I respect him. He is my *sempai* (senior) in Japan." He is also generous in his praise of the Japanese employees at IBM Japan. "Without them and without our long history of commitment to Japan, we would not be where we are today," he says. These are simple words, but they are words American managers in Japan must remember to say and mean.

IBM Japan's Future

IBM Japan has a good record, but it has not been completely fumble free. Among its mistakes were (1) preoccupation with large mainframe computers resulting in delayed introduction of personal computers, and (2) an inadequate distribution system due to preoccupation with direct and rental sales.

IBM Japan's debut in the personal computer field was its IBM multistation 5550. Developed by its Fujisawa laboratories, it offered three types of functions: a Japanese language word processor, personal computer and intelligent terminal, all with *kanji* capabilities. However, its 1983 introduction was at least six months behind its competitors, thus conceding an important market share to NEC and Fujitsu. Sales were also hampered at first because of inadequate means of distribution and a higher price tag than other systems.

Since 1983, however, IBM Japan's strategy has been to outdo its Japanese rivals, and to do so in a way more Japanese than Japanese themselves can be. If previously remote from common customers, it was determined not to be viewed as such by the Japanese public, and its campaign was a vigorous one. For example:

1. It has enlisted outside help to market its low-cost high-volume product lines. Independent companies of different specialties are now serving as IBM's *dairiten* or distributors. In addition, IBM product dealers for over-the-counter sales are also appointed across the nation.

2. It maintains IBM OA (office automation) Centers in major cities throughout the country to give assistance to personal computer owners, including classes, technical assistance and lessons for children. It also supports IBM OA club activities.

3. It has created two RETAIN (remote technological assessment information network) Centers for speedy and accurate maintenance activities.

4. It now goes to classrooms and promotes computer fairs in schools. These activities are conducted with the introduction of its JX personal computer series, in the expanded small- and very small-size product range.

5. The number of IBM employees has been increased by more than a thousand each year. The majority of these new employees are systems engineers or systems engineer trainees, reaffirming the company's commitment to customer service.

IBM Japan is not a vertically integrated company and must purchase parts from domestic and foreign suppliers. For its size, it has not had affiliated companies to support its various activities. In the past several years, this situation has changed drastically. It has joined forces with Kanematsu Gosho, a major trading company, to extend its global sales network. Domestically, sales activities are supported by other IBM Japan subsidiaries such as IBM Japan Sales Co. and Computer Systems

Leasing, Ltd. The names of some of its subsidiaries illustrate its focus for future development, for example, Advanced Systems Technology Development, Inc. and Systems Development, Ltd.

In November 1983, IBM Japan, Mitsubishi Trading and Cosmo Eighty became partners in establishing a subsidiary, AST, and a related subsidiary, AST Research Institute. These two subsidiaries will engage in research activities on INS (information network system), develop hardware and software and otherwise study information processing and communications-related technologies. By the year 2000, the newly privatized NTT (Nippon Telegraph and Telephone) plans to complete INS across Japan. Through this and other arrangements, IBM Japan is poised to be part of the most ambitious information networking of the century. It makes good business sense to create related companies to pursue common goals. Should there be an objection on the grounds that IBM is a foreign company, the interlocking nature of these arrangements would lessen the likelihood of such an objection.

The future does look good for IBM Japan in several areas. It has an advantage in large mainframe computers, the ones being used to create simulations for the future and determine government policies. For example, IBM Japan has been able to predict the needs of Hyogo prefecture for the coming fifty years in a program called Hyogo Dynamics. More of this type of service will be required, and Japanese governmental bureaus seem more willing now to adopt IBM systems.

As the hub of IBM's Asia/Pacific Group, IBM Japan has been providing technical assistance to those countries requiring *kanji* keyboards. Taiwan has one version of Chinese, Beijing, yet another, and in South Korea, there is *hangul* script. In personal computers, the technology of the IBM 5550 can be transferred immediately. The fact that IBM has a larger worldwide network than any of its closest rivals, such as Fujitsu, is an advantage. In fact, in the People's Republic of China, the computer to be produced locally is the IBM 5550. In South Korea, its IBM subsidiary had a 50 percent a year growth.

Problems still remain, however. In an unlikely time in the future, assuming that there is another shortage of memory chips, how can a company like IBM Japan cope? Must it take the road of almost full vertical integration as many Japanese companies have done? IBM Japan's ability to purchase parts competitively has been one factor in its decidedly favorable balance sheet. Japanese suppliers, however, have given preferential delivery of newly developed semiconductors to their in-house computer divisions. Assuming Japanese computer companies benefit from another technological breakthrough like the display of a 256K RAM by NTT in 1979, will IBM Japan or IBM itself be prepared? The question extends beyond the borders of Japan. Can the American computer industry allow its Japanese competitors to retain an edge in memory chips?

IBM Japan can remain a strong company if, in spite of its size, it can retain the "small company attitude" and not forget the basics, namely its seven-article corporate philosophy. A note of caution is necessary, however, in its view on "responsibility toward stockholders." In the past, special arrangements were needed to repatriate its profits to WTC headquarters. In this chapter, the impressive performance of IBM Japan's profit column has been compared with Fujitsu's. Sometimes, however, victory belongs to those who deny today's profit in order to obtain tomorrow's advantage. Fujitsu is a formidable competitor, and so is NEC, because of this attitude. Is IBM prepared to face them five or ten years from now?

COCA COLA

Coca Cola owes its growth to Japan's foreign exchange law and unfriendly Japanese officials, as much as to its managerial skills.

Coca Cola entered Japan in 1946, the year after the war, to provide soft drinks for American GIs in Japan. After the occupation, the company retained its Japan operations. In 1956, a man by the name of Takanashi Nisaburo bought out one of its Tokyo plants to start his own bottling company. The company had other plants around the country but they were uneconomical to operate and, after the sale of the Tokyo plant, all except the Tsurumi plant were closed. In 1957, the Coca Cola Company of Japan was established. It was one of the so-called yen companies; foreigners could invest freely with converted foreign funds but could not repatriate their earnings. The Japanese economy was still in the process of recovery and the government regulated all flow of goods.

In those days, Japan's soft drink business was handled by hundreds of small bottlers. The government, fearing that the new company might dislocate some of these small bottlers, insisted that Coca Cola charge an exorbitantly high price. It reasoned that the price would be an adequate safeguard against its market penetration. Japan's traditional soft drink had been of one variety, a clear cider-like beverage. It was also felt that Coca Cola's dark coloring and medicinal taste would drive away most potential customers.

Government officials were wrong, however. In spite of its price, which had been set so high that it did not have to be modified for fifteen years, it sold well. The company would have cut the price, but the bureaucrats would not allow it. Unable to repatriate its earnings, which were increasing at a rate completely unanticipated, the company had the pleasant task of figuring out how to spend them.

The profits were first reinvested in distribution. Between 1960 and 1963, fifteen bottlers were founded. These bottlers were selected not because of their prior experience in the soft drink industry but because of their enthusiasm. They had to be prominent citizens well respected by the local community. The community-oriented approach had its immediate payoff in the form of availability of bank loans and the ease with which the plant site could be selected.

Departing from conventional wisdom, the company adopted a marketing method called the direct route sales system. It meant that cash had to be paid and nothing sold under consignment. The soft drink had to be sold directly to distributors, including those in "mom-and-pop" stores. Some of the bottlers were apprehensive about this practice but followed the company's lead.

The system required a substantial outlay of money to train company employees, but at that time it was not an issue.

The second part of the investment was in the promotion campaign. The company spent generously in television and radio commercials. The phrase *Sukatto sawayaka Coca Cola* (What a great feeling — this Coca Cola) became the best-known television line in the 1960s through the early part of the 1970s. The word *sawayaka* is now the title of the company's monthly magazine, which contains articles about nature, travel, poetry and other topics of interest, with only two pages in each issue devoted to vignettes of Coca Cola history. It is soft selling at its best, and the magazine has regular paid subscribers.

Success brought further success. As the advertising campaign progressed, consumption became even greater. Fanta was introduced in 1958, offering a variety previously unavailable in Japan. In 1964, the year of the Tokyo Olympics, when the yen was made convertible, Coca Cola already topped the list of soft drinks in market share. By the end of the 1960s, profits in Japan came to represent about a quarter of Coca Cola's worldwide earnings. In 1972, Coca Cola Japan became a member of the *Keidanren* (Federation of Economic Associations), the first foreign-owned firm to attain that distinction.

The company has had keen eyes and ears serving its own interest as well as the community's. There was an overproduction of *mikan* (tangerines) in 1972 and 1973. Importing from its parent company the technology that developed Hi-C, Coca Cola Japan succeeded in creating *mikan*-flavored Hi-C.

In some ways, Coca Cola retains its foreign identity more so than many other American companies in Japan. There have been eight presidents since 1957, when the company was formally established, yet only one Japanese, M. Iwamura, served as president (from December 1971 to September 1975.) To company employees this is an accepted part of working for Coca Cola. Presidents come and go, but employees endure. They are content with their company's performance and its excellent public acceptance.

The key to Coca Cola's success, however, is not so much in its American top management as its ability to forge a strong partnership with its bottlers, who are independent franchise owners. There are now seventeen bottlers and territories, operated by some of Japan's most respected companies. For example, Tone Coca Cola Bottling Company is owned by Kikkoman; Mikuni Bottling is publicly owned with Mitsubishi Trading having the majority share; and Fuji Bottling is owned jointly by Mitsubishi Trading and Meidiya. These companies individually and jointly represent an enormous accumulation of knowledge about Japanese business, and one's learning curve is shortened considerably when working with them. Coca Cola Japan's marketing system is unique. It works well because each franchisee is responsible for the distribution system in its territory while maintaining close ties with its local distributors.

The benefit, however, runs in both directions. Coca Cola Japan provides these independent franchisees with personnel training and technological assistance. A large number of Japanese personnel have been sent overseas for management training by Coca Cola Japan. Independent franchisees are members of the Coca Cola Bottlers Association. Normally, members of Mitsui and Mitsubishi Trading are competitors and seldom meet to discuss business. Under the umbrella of Coca Cola, they all meet, compare notes and engage in the joint effort of promoting Coca Cola products. Without intending to, Coca Cola's management practice has added something to the fabric of Japanese society.

Having its own distribution system, Coca Cola Japan has been able to keep up with shifts in customer preferences. The sales figures it accumulates are not just statistics. In helping a local "mom-and-pop" store owner put a case of Coke on his shelf, a driver knows how the products are sold. With the "small company attitude," the company maintains, local distributors' experiences are made known. Sizes of Japan's Coke bottles and cans are different from those found in the United States. From the notion of what is the optimum amount for a customer to consume to the shelf height and width in local groceries, different factors were considered before these Japanese sizes were determined. Coca Cola Japan was spared the embarrassment of introducing the New Coke. The "classic" Coke gave the company its start in Japan, and the public still likes it. That is the only brand sold in Japan, even though concession is made to the now weight conscious Japanese with a Cola Light brand.

REFLECTIONS

IBM and Coca Cola have succeeded in Japan with determination and a keen sense of what the customers needed. Success came in spite of the Japanese bureaucrats' discriminatory treatment in favor of their own domestic industries. For American companies thinking of entering the Japanese market, this is a sobering thought. Bureaucratic barriers may exist but they cannot keep out indefinitely good products manufactured and managed by good companies.

IBM and Coca Cola have been in Japan longer, and that is to their advantage. For other companies, though, it simply means that to succeed, they must be willing to make a long-term commitment in Japan. It also means that they must be willing to invest in Japan: investing in human resources, distribution systems, and plants. The home office must be willing to allow its Japanese subsidiary to grow on its own, delegating to it the power to make decisions, allowing it to enter into cooperative endeavors and partnership arrangements with Japanese companies, and sacrificing today's profits for tomorrow's market share. The following is a quick checklist for companies contemplating entry into the Japanese market:

Is my company willing to make a long-term commitment to the Japanese market?
- We are willing to forego profits for _____ years.
- We encourage reinvestment in the Japanese market over repatriation of the profits.

· We are willing to allow our Japanese subsidiary to retain ____ percent of its annual profit for reinvestment for ____ years.

Is my company willing to delegate power to its Japanese subsidiary?
· We plan to name a Japanese national as its chief executive officer
within ____ years.
· We plan to have a member of the Japanese subsidiary installed as a
director of our board.

Does my company plan to utilize existing distribution channels?
· If so, what modifications may be needed?
· If it chooses to establish its own distribution system, has it thought
about the following options:
— Purchase existing distribution companies?
— Subcontract Japanese distributors?

Is my company willing to enter into a joint venture with a Japanese com-
pany?
· Do we have established criteria in selecting a potential partner?
· Are these criteria flexible enough to accommodate peculiarities of
the Japanese market?
· When conflict arises, do we resort to:
— Arbitration?
— Law suits?
— Or intense discussion?

In entering the Japanese market, my company plans to enlist help from
the following:
· U.S. government, including the Tokyo embassy.
· Japanese government, including its consular and Japan External
Trade Organization officials.
· My state's representative in Tokyo.
· Major Japanese banks.

A few words of explanation are necessary on the matter of
conflict resolution. Japan is not a litigious society and lawsuits
are absolutely the last resort. There are no winners. One may
score a point only to lose long-term friends and contacts. If dis-
agreement surfaces, talk things over. In Japanese there is a term,
hanashiai. Though it is not an exact translation, "come now, and
let us reason together" (Isaiah 1:18) comes close to its intent.

In your initial contact with Japan, you may find your state

representative in Tokyo useful. He can provide you with necessary introductions, but do not forget to get help from Japanese banks. As lenders and main banks, they have been involved with the affairs of Japanese companies more deeply than most U.S. banks dream possible, and their introductions can create useful contacts.

When you are in Japan establishing your business, do not hesitate to share with your Japanese employees your deeply felt convictions. Let them know what your company's goals and aspirations are. Create a sense of trust that can bind you and your Japanese employees together. Create a good team. A member of the crew of U.S.S. *Stars and Stripes*, facing the challenge of the America's Cup race, talked about how to win in the sport: "It's good to have tradition and values on your side. And there are three principles of how to win. The first is attitude, the second is attitude, and the third is attitude." It is also a good formula for success for an American company in Japan.

CHAPTER 8

The United States and Japan

"**Y**oung man, there is America — which at this day serves for little more than to amuse you with stories of savage men and uncouth manners; yet shall, before you taste of death, show itself equal to the whole of that commerce which now attracts the envy of the world," said Edmund Burke in 1775 at the Parliament, urging conciliation with America. More than two centuries have passed since that British statesman spoke these words, but the very essence of what he said can still hold true. With America's huge trade and federal deficits placed alongside their country's industrial wealth, some Japanese businessmen predict the demise of America's power. They cite street crime in New York and the lack of will to work by multiracial workers as proof positive of their assertion. Yet to paraphrase Mark Twain, news of the early demise of America is premature.

Vitality still remains in America. Take the case of Nucor, whose specialty steel operations we discussed earlier. Another example may be found in IBM, whose Lexington, Kentucky plant is fully rationalized, not just in line works carried out with sophisticated automated machines, but also in the way supplies are received. The number of vendors has been cut drastically and those remaining now subject themselves to tight quality control measures. Its sister plant in Charlotte, North Carolina, produces Proprinter, which has captured 18 percent of the computer-printer market.

In a market previously dominated by the Japanese import, instead of continuing to import modified Epsons, Big Blue decided to go on its own and succeeded. A key ingredient in this success story was the ability of people to work together. According to product manager Charles J. Rogers, "The manufacturing people literally shared the same coffee machine as the design people." In removing cumbersome springs, screws and pulleys not absolutely necessary for the manufacture of the printer — which incidentally would aid in automation — designers had to consult line workers and vice versa.[1]

When things do not go as planned, a pending crisis can be turned into an opportunity. In 1982, Lincoln Electric Company of Cleveland experienced a drop in sales of 28 percent from the previous year. Fifty of its employees decided to go on the road to sell the company's small welder, the SP200 used in small machine shops and auto body shops. They knew the machine was good and impressed customers with their enthusiasm. Close contact with customers also helped them understand how their products are viewed. They received no compensation except car mileage. The education they received was invaluable, however, and similar in many ways to that once experienced by Mazda and Matsushita employees.[2]

Cummins Engine discovered in 1984 that two of its key customers, Navistar and Freightliner, were considering the purchase of low-priced Japanese engines. The company answered with a 30 percent price cut, thus saving its market share and jobs. Instead of earning profits through higher prices, it now relies on rationalization and tighter quality control. Quality control is also a key phrase for Cypress. That company has introduced flexibility in semiconductor manufacturing by changing its machines frequently to make different chips. It has an edge over Japanese competitors because of this very flexibility, which the Japanese have not really considered.[3]

Lutron Electronic is a privately owned company with about 400 employees, making illumination equipment for hotels and convention centers. Its sales people return frequently to the two plants in Allentown, Pennsylvania to see what is made and chat with the company president. There is no barrier between white- and blue-collar workers. One Cambridge-educated engineer went there for a summer job and decided to stay: "I love this place," he said. "It's informal, friendly and very efficient."

Stories like these abound across the country. If there is anything disquieting about them, however, it is that they are merely pockets of excellence. In many other areas, productivity remains elusive. Moreover, in searching for parts, these excellent companies cannot always rely on other American companies.

A CASE FOR BEING HUNGRY

Honda Electronics, whose products include sophisticated body scanners, can obtain any machine or raw material it needs within the five-kilometer radius of the city of Toyohashi where it is located. When supplies reach them, quality is assured. This means that the company can proceed with any project within thirty minutes after deciding to undertake it. It does not need a large inventory on hand. It is almost like having a just-in-time system of delivery, and this applies even to new projects. When different industries grow side by side as in Toyohashi's case, improvement in one tends to have an important multiplier effect on others.

Toyohashi has a national Institute of Technology that is on the cutting edge of high technology. Students in computer engineering, for example, learn how to cut the silicon wafer and make it into a silicon chip using machines donated by NEC. Takahashi Akira, the city's mayor, is a former speaker of the unicameral Aichi Prefectural Assembly and an honorary citizen of Paris. When the city council or Chamber of Commerce meets, they speak of the city's growth in worldwide terms. The city's local paper, *Higashi Echo Shimbun*, gives prominence to both regional and national economic news.

The city is unique in having a technology institute. When it comes to supporting growth for all sectors, however, Toyohashi is hardly alone. Kushiro, a seaport in Hokkaido, has a balanced development program that includes a modern paper mill while retaining traditional sectors such as fishing and coal mining. Its local paper, *Kushiro Shimbun*, gives sophisticated coverage of economic development, informing and educating local citizens. Iyo Mishima, on the island of Shikoku, has already been discussed in connection with Taio Paper.

The ability of local communities to have sustained growth has been one of the telling signs of Japan's current economic strength. In contrast, in the United States, too often a local community's economy is influenced by the closing of one plant. One thing leads to another, from the expanding unemployment roll to the closing of downtown stores accompanied by further deterioration of the industrial sector, which finally results in a slow death for the region's economy. The town may try to attract another industry but, with one failure, others seem to avoid the region. The tale of these cities has no happy ending in America. This is so even though in terms of raw materials, other resources, and attractiveness of its market America still has more to offer than its competitors.

Many reasons have been offered to explain this phenomenon. Government policies may be responsible, in view of the staggering federal and trade deficits. Unions attack management for its inability to plan ahead; management in turn, may blame unions for greed and workers' general lack of commitment. Then there is a claim that America has somehow lost its work ethic. Paul McCracken, former presidential adviser, once said, "If John Calvin came back to earth, the nation he would feel most comfortable in would be Japan, that is where his real children would be."[4]

The desire to excel that characterized America's past seems now to reside in Japan. For executives, closing down a plant in town X may not mean much. By outsourcing the same products they probably could bring their company's profit up by 10 percent the next year. When the company is in real trouble, they can still expect a generous settlement from the company for severance. Workers too may be resigned to their fate and look forward to severance pay. In short, there has been no true incentive not to close down the plant. Life is still tolerable even after the closing. Somehow, America has succeeded in institutionalizing a system that invariably leads to failure, and there is no penalty for it.

"Be Hungry — Without It There Can Be No Growth"

The will to succeed is an elusive concept because it cannot be quantified. Yet its presence or absence can make a great deal of difference. "Be hungry — without it there can be no growth," says Inamori Kazuo, founder of Kyocera. His IC packages made of fine ceramics have been used in the space shuttle Columbia. With the resumption of the shuttle program, Kyocera is expected to do well. From 7 employees in 1959 to about 13,000 today, Kyocera has advanced by leaps and bounds, and behind it all, is that spirit of hunger that has been inculcated in the minds of its workers.

By conventional standards, Inamori was not destined for success. His earlier days were dotted with a series of failures. He wanted to enter Kagoshima's First Middle School and failed the entrance examination twice. He applied to the College of Medicine at Osaka University and was rejected. He was forced to go to the engineering faculty of Kagoshima University, nicknamed a "lunch-box university" because one could come and go freely and no prestige was attached to its diploma. On graduation, he sought employment with Teikoku Sekiyu (Imperial Oil) and was rejected. He ended up with a Shofu, a small Kyoto company in the inorganic chemistry field. It was a company that seldom showed a profit, but while working there Inamori became aware of the importance of new materials, such as ceramics. Pursuit of this new material led to the founding of his own company, Kyocera.

Inamori is distinguished by his vision and drive. As he writes his company philosophy today, he does not allow his employees to remain complacent: "We started from nothing and have reached this plateau. But as we start anew, we still consider ourselves as having nothing.... Effort is limitless; when an individual is willing to make a limitless effort, he is surprised to discover his own potentials."[5] Self-reliant, determined and above all hungry for success, Inamori has turned himself and his colleagues into a dedicated group that has produced the Kyocera of today.

To hunger for a cause may be the one thing that separates success from failure.

POSSIBLE SOLUTIONS

If we desire a resurgent America, not in rhetoric but in reality, we must motivate our people and restore productivity in all industrial sectors. With this in mind, we can now judge the effectiveness of the measures taken or proposed either by the government or the private sector.

Industrial Policy for America?

One suggestion often heard is to create an industrial policy for the United States. Robert B. Reich, a management professor at Harvard, maintains that a rational industrial policy must be developed to assist research and development, to nurture key infant industries and to help identify key linkage industries such as steel, which as a basic commodity can influence the pricing and strengths of other industries. To promote exports, he suggests providing export insurance covering commercial and political risks. Indeed, such a policy would be an improvement over the current hodgepodge of nonpolicy, which includes "voluntary" restrictions on imports. Professor Reich is careful in suggesting that he does not believe in creating a large bureaucracy to administer his industrial policy, and speaks admiringly of Japan's MITI, with only about 2,500 professional members in the ministry.[6]

Starting from different premises, Ezra Vogel, a Harvard Japanologist, comes to a somewhat similar conclusion and suggests that two bodies be established as mechanisms for coordination of various policies to enhance U.S. competitiveness. The two bodies are The National Competitiveness Council, to be established in the White House, and a semi-independent National Economic Cooperation Council.[7]

The goals mentioned by Reich and Vogel are praiseworthy ones we can fully share. However, the intrusion of bureaucracy, unpretentious as it may seem at first sight, is fraught with danger. For one thing, the speed needed to solve trade issues is missing. By the time solutions are given, enough damage may already have been done to the industries affected to render the solutions meaningless. The suggested White House Council is not likely to receive operational responsibilities, especially after the Iranian arms deal crisis. It can easily become another layer of Washington bureaucracy, its existence a cause for additional delays.

People who see bureaucracy as a solution may be reminded that one of the major policy aims of Prime Minister Nakasone is administrative reform, including privatization of a number of government-owned industries. To sustain further economic growth, Japan has discovered that the pervasive power of its bureaucracy must be lessened. It is hardly the time for America to take an opposite course.

Less Government = Greater Efficiency:
Examples from Japan

In April 1987, Japan's national railway system (JNR) was transferred to a number of regional companies to operate.

Following the privatization of the NTT two years earlier, the goverment gave a clear message that the private sector, not government, should manage the nation's economy. The JNR had lost money except on two lines: the bullet superexpress from Tokyo to Hakata and the Yamanote circle line within Tokyo. Privatization was intended to infuse private capital and initiatives, both sorely needed. Prior to this privatization, services in a number of the most unprofitable lines were cut. Some of them were transferred to private hands earlier and showed a remarkable transformation.

The Amagi line from Amagi in Fukuoka and Motoyama in Saga is only fourteen kilometers long. It was turned over to a private company in April 1986. The company created new parking facilities, increased services from seven to thirty-two daily round trips between the two cities, and made transfer into another private line, Nishitetsu, possible. Passengers suddenly found that commuting to the city of Fukuoka became much easier. While operated by the JNR the line was a money loser, but with riders increasing by 300 percent under new management, the company is now financially sound. When it first started, it asked for private donations to maintain the railway. Although a controversial move, 8,337 local residents responded. Through this act of contributing, they can always claim that the railway is "theirs," and this pride of "ownership" is reflected in continued local support for the company.

The Sanriku railway company was started in April 1984, the very first year of the privatization movement. It is situated in the Iwate prefecture in the northern part of Honshu. Operating two unconnected rail lines of 71 and 36.6 kilometers each, it was feared that the company would never take off financially because the two lines were poorly utilized. The private company upgraded its services and in the first year carried 2.68 million passengers to make a sizable profit.

It was the story of the little railway company that could, and proved to the country that privatization would work in maintaining essential services. Employees were willing to work for less. Former JNR employees who were pensioned off were willing to come back to work for a small supplement to their retirement pay. Passengers who had utilized these lines both under the JNR and the private company could see the difference. The people working there remained the same, but their attitudes were strikingly different.

Currency Realignment — Why It Does Not Work

The privatization of JNR worked because it brought into Japan's railway system private initiatives accompanied by changes in the attitudes of its workers. Any measure — public or private — that attempts to foster an attitude of complacency, however, is doomed to failure. Seen in this light, the joint currency intervention by the finance ministers of five nations initiated on September 22, 1985, can be considered one of the most ill-advised measures undertaken by these economic powers.

The realignment accomplished its stated purposes of lowering the overvalued U.S. dollar, raising the undervalued yen, and for the time being preventing the U.S. Congress from enacting protectionist legislation. Preoccupied by the trade deficit and exchange rate figures, the finance ministers entered into a political agreement without carefully studying the economic consequences of their actions. Briefly, their work resulted in the following:

1. With the sharp rise in the value of its currency, Japan suddenly found itself controlling 60 percent of the world's capital assets by the end of 1986. Eight of the ten largest banks in the world are now Japanese. The U.S. financial market has thus become deeply dependent on Japanese capital. "Are the Japanese buying?" becomes one of the most important questions asked at each Treasury bill auction.

2. The U.S. trade gap with Japan has widened, and there is

no end in sight. It is true that in the yen amount, the gap narrowed in the year 1986, but in terms of the dollar it increased by over $8 billion to a record $58 billion. The overall U.S. trade deficit for that year was about $170 billion.

3. Some Japanese industries heavily dependent on exports, such as steel and electric appliances, are beginning to show signs of difficulty. No compensating advantages are received by their U.S. counterparts, however.

4. In machine tools and car parts, Japanese products are so deeply embedded in the U.S. market that there is little likelihood of their being replaced by U.S. products in spite of their rising costs.

5. The nations benefitting from the currency realignment are those newly industrialized countries of the Pacific Rim, especially South Korea and Taiwan, whose currencies were allowed to fall along with the U.S. dollar, thus maintaining their products' price advantages not only in the United States but in the rest of the world.

6. In the manufacturing sector, U.S. exports have generally not been able to compete successfully against Japanese products and those of the Pacific Rim nations. U.S. corporations also have continued their practice of outsourcing — nowadays joined by some Japanese companies — in the Pacific Rim nations, thus further negating any advantage that might have arisen through the current realignment.

7. Meanwhile, in spite of the fall in the value of the dollar, the agriculture export market did not recover. Some importing nations found new supply sources while others, such as India, were quickly becoming self-sufficient in agricultural products.

The tragedy in the currency realignment policy is that it hurts both the United States and Japan without redressing any of the problems it was intended to solve. Fortunately, the currency realignment has not resulted in steep inflation for the United States in part due to falling oil prices and a world economy generally saturated with commodities. This condition cannot continue, however. The policy has also fostered another round of complacency — progress and productivity's worst enemy. The dollar's lower value has allowed those import-sensitive sectors in the U.S. to raise their prices without fear of losing their market share. Without managing their companies well or raising their productivity, some companies can still claim a good quarterly performance; they are subsisting on an empty dream. Companies whose profits are based on the temporary benefit of the currency realignment are houses built on sand, and they cannot long endure.

Private Sector Can Also Make Mistakes

The government is not alone in making bad judgments. The private sector is hardly immune. In explaining its friendly takeover by GE, RCA announced that it was taking this step in order "to generate the critical mass essential in continued leadership in a global economy." It expressed a hope that through this critical mass, the new company could cut development and marketing costs and move more aggressively in the world market. Critical mass in itself, however, is not a guarantee of quality. If the newly formed giant forms a bureaucratic network without corresponding productivity gains, if it does not share information adequately or if it stifles creativity, then the two companies might better have remained separate.

One wants to wish the merged GE well, but its actions do not show much future promise. In January 1987, it began to trim its manufacturing operations, closing down a number of plants across the country. It obviously has not learned from its past experience. Over two decades ago, GE gave up manufacturing television sets and started distributing Japanese-made TVs. Since then it has not kept up with the latest technologies, and today, even if it wants to, GE probably cannot produce a television set competitive with foreign products. It may obtain profits without production, but abandoning manufacturing is not just the loss of jobs for workers. It means loss of a specific technology and a lengthened learning curve for the industry in the future.

In our fumble-free management, a company must meet the test of being community-, customer-, and employee-oriented. Of these three criteria, GE fails in two. If the decision is only confined to one company, it is not particularly significant. When these private decisions are collectively applied, however, as a nation, we face industrial decline.

In the Gospel of Matthew, a man about to travel to a far country gave five talents to one servant, two to another and one to the third. The first two invested the money wisely and, on their master's return, each repaid him double the amount received. The third hid the one talent in the earth and returned it to the master. Now let us assume that the three servants had acted differently — the first one doing nothing with the money while the remaining two doubled their income. On the master's return, the first servant would have five talents, the second four and the third two.

This is the parallel we may draw to illustrate the relative positions of the United States, Japan and the newly industrialized nations of the Pacific Basin. The danger that lurks for the United States is in its uncaring attitude. We have riches others envy, but if these riches are merely used for nonproductive purposes, what is there to gain? Meanwhile, once resource-poor nations like Japan have surpassed us in many areas, while South Korea and others inch closer and closer to the attainment level we now possess. If we do not want to be left behind, we must take steps to reindustrialize America.

RESTRUCTURING THE AMERICAN ECONOMY

What are the steps we can take to bring about American resurgence? Here, perhaps, the steps taken by the Japanese can serve as a point of reference.

Strategic Protectionism

The Japanese practice has been one of strategic protectionism, protecting an industrial sector considered important for the nation's well-being and delaying entry of foreign products into Japan to allow that industry to grow. This has been carried out even in the face of foreign pressures for liberalization. Technology and capital are concentrated in developing this sector, and once it becomes competitive, liberalization occurs. By then, however, Japan has a competitive advantage with its economies of scale and can penetrate the world market.

Publicly Japan adheres to free trade, but it has enough foresight to know when to engage in protectionism. In a sense, the Japanese have been good students of Alexander Hamilton. They have known that to acquire "a new and useful branch of industry" is to create a "permanent addition to the general stock of productive labor."[8]

In contrast, successive American administrations have adhered to "free trade" with disastrous consequences for the American economy. Free trade is generally supported today by the agricultural sector, which benefits from the sale of its products overseas and the decline in value of the dollar. Free trade is supported by consumer groups that insist on the right to the best products at the lowest cost. Free trade is supported by some economists and most editorial writers. As a policy, however, it is unworkable.

In practice, America is not a "free trade" nation when it must rely on the so-called orderly marketing agreements, trigger-price mechanism or voluntary restraints. These measures have simply shifted the burden of administering trade protection to other countries and created a basis for future retaliation. These are policies haphazardly conceived and implemented. They have failed to stem the flow of goods to the United States and to protect the industries for whom they were intended. The ideological desire to be true to Adam Smith's 1776 theory thus creates an invisible fetter on the American people, denying them the freedom to seek economic growth and expansion.

The problem is not new. Tension existed between the advocates of free trade and protectionism even during the early days of the Republic. There was Alexander Hamilton, whose celebrated Report on Manufactures in 1791 strongly advocated imposition of protective tariffs. Congress gave this report a cold reception, and allowed the nation's profligate consumption of foreign goods to continue. Then there was Thomas Jefferson, whose personal affinity with the notion of laissez faire was tempered with a desire to create an "American system" of tariffs and other aids to assist domestic manufactures. America's subsequent development as an industrial nation has shown the wisdom of utilizing Hamiltonian means (protectionism) to reach the ultimate Jeffersonian goals (laissez faire). This lesson of history must not be forgotten as we contemplate the future.

Kiuchi Nobutane's Nation Building

The Japanese people do not have theoretical hangups and therefore come up with more rational solutions. Kiuchi Nobutane is currently president of the Institute of World Economy and informally serves as an adviser to successive Japanese prime ministers. He views economic activities as necessary for "nation building and to enhance the national identity." Starting from this premise, he offers the following principles for economic conduct:[9]

1. Do not force upon other nations the principle of "free trade." Each country may engage in "free trade to the degree it desires."

2. Free trade means "to strengthen domestic industries by letting them be exposed to the wind of foreign competition." Ultimately it must be pursued for the benefit of the importing nation, and any benefit accrued to the exporting nation must be incidental. In the postwar era, somehow this principle has been misinterpreted to mean that free trade is for the benefit of exporting nations. This must be rectified promptly.

3. Emphasis must be placed on the "freedom of nation build-

ing," not on economic development through movement of commodities among nations. It is only through "freedom of nation building" that any nation can maintain "its own values and national identity" and assume "self-responsibility." This indeed is the best basis for a new world order, and this principle must be adhered to at all times and at all costs.

Today, Kiuchi is not alone in thinking of the peril of excessive exports by Japan and excessive imports by the United States. Others fully appreciate the need to have a strong America and are ready to impose self-restraints on Japan if necessary. They would prefer, however, that such initiatives come from the United States. In fact, they would not object to America protecting some of its industries through customs levies, because both countries would benefit in the end.

Japanese industrialists' enlightened views on protectionism may be seen in the advice that Inayama Yoshihiro, as president of the Keidanren, gave to Chinese leaders in 1985. China had had a favorable balance of trade toward Japan until around 1983 when things quickly reversed to the tune of about $2 billion. They wanted to solve this problem by asking Japan to import more.

Inayama reminisced about the days when Japan was still rebuilding its economy. "We didn't have television, refrigerators or central heating. We worked and saved and banks lent our money to the industries," he said. "Don't you think you are allowing too much temptation today? You allow your people to buy televisions and refrigerators. It may be difficult to stop importing these commodities, but you have a government capable of doing this." In his view, most countries do not dare suppress imports for fear of consumer disapproval. That of course is not the way of nation building. Inayama had himself experienced a bitter loss on a steel sale to China as president of New Japan Steel because of China's import restrictions. For the sake of the host country, however, such measures must be taken.[10]

Kiuchi and Inayama suggest that the United States impose customs duties if necessary. In the meantime, Japan is prepared to impose export taxes if needed. These views have never surfaced in the United States, due in part to the American editorial writers' prejudice against anything giving credence to protectionism and in part to the scarcity of good translated works. Not knowing these views, administration spokesmen suggest continuously that the United States not impose customs duties for fear of retaliation. What Japanese leaders actually fear most are not customs levies, but the inability of America to address its trade imbalances. They, like the Americans, seek an America whose economy is stable and can continue to sustain economic growth in the world.

Limited Protection for American Industries

With these points in mind, the following modest suggestions are made:

1. Congress should identify strategic and linkage industries whose continued existence is essential for the defense and well-being of the nation.

2. In defining what will constitute strategic and linkage industries, Congress must observe the following criteria:

Is this a basic industry without which the nation's defense or well-being may be threatened? Steel may be considered one sector under this category. It is still the basic commodity with which many other products are made, and in wartime the nation cannot survive without it.

Is the technology represented by this industry so vital that protection is necessary? Microchips and other high-tech items may come under this category. Can we have a viable space program without the technology to carry it out? Can we always depend on our Japanese suppliers to produce sensitive materials? If supplies are cut, what are other alternatives? America needs these technologies within its own borders.

Furthermore, some new technologies require enormous startup costs. The government must be prepared to give them protection.

The above criteria are simple ones. When applied without prejudice, they will not allow industries such as shoes and textiles to be designated as strategic or linkage industries.

3. When these strategic or linkage industries find themselves unable to compete, they may seek protection in the form of customs levies on foreign products. These levies are not to exceed three years, and if after three years conditions do not improve, the levies must be allowed to lapse with no second application allowed.

The three-year limit is imposed to make certain that no industry will become "fat" under customs levies protection. For the purpose of this book, it also means that companies seeking this type of protection must immediately implement the fumble-free management method.

No company outsourcing the majority of its productive facilities overseas may claim protection under this provision. On certain categories of products, the United States may seek bilateral agreements with Japan and other allies to restrict importation to the United States through quotas or export duties. However, preference must always be on U.S.-imposed customs duties. They can be applied more impartially and discourage outsourcing since duties will be imposed equally on parts imported into this country.

4. In the event that the trade balance does not improve, Congress may impose an emergency levy of no longer than three years on all nonessential imports.

These are simple measures, which incidentally do not contain steps toward retaliation. This is because they are not intended as tools for trade friction but for preserving productivity for America. Questions may be raised about the danger of infringing on the provisions of the General Agreements on Tariffs and Trade (GATT) formed in 1948. Under international law, however, according to the rule *rebus sic stantibus*, a treaty is binding as long as the relevant facts and circumstances remain essentially the same. America and the world have changed very much since 1948. It is time for the United States to take the lead in revising and adjusting the provisions of GATT to benefit all concerned.

COMPETITION FOR THE FUTURE

These simple suggestions also answer the problems posed by a 1985 presidential commission on industrial competitiveness. It reported that our inattention to manufacturing had cost us dearly in television, automobile and machine tool industries. It predicted that the next would be the semiconductor industry. "It does us little good to design state-of-the-art products," says the commission report, "if within a short time our foreign competitors can manufacture them more cheaply." A modest measure of protection as suggested is thus called for.

The warnings sounded by the commission make one ponder the industrial future of our two countries, the United States and Japan. To use the football parlance, we are two teams bound for the Super Bowl. The United States is strong in passing and has a superior quarterback known for his ability to throw a "Hail Mary" touchdown pass (read our state-of-the-art innovations). The offense, however, is poor in running games (read our inability to penetrate Japanese and other foreign markets); our defense tends to give up too much territory (read the invasion of the U.S. market by Japan). The Japanese team may take all four downs to go ten yards (read their initial difficulty in competing against the United States; remember John Foster Dulles, who once said to the Japanese, "You can hardly sell us anything we need"). They make more first downs (read televisions, cameras, household appliances, automobiles), however, and they reach the end zone (read the $49.7 billion surplus in 1985 and $58 billion in 1986). Their defense is tough and physical, and they prefer a five-yard penalty rather than conceding an inch when the other team attacks (read their tariff and nontariff barriers and liberalization measures under pressure).

If you are betting, which team do you pick to win the Super Bowl? It is time to restructure our team with fumble-free management, and a word to the wise is sufficient.

A Common Sense Approach to Japanese Etiquette

Many business deals can go awry if the American visiting his counterpart in Japan does not know how to behave properly. The Japanese word for etiquette is *reigi*, which means to be respectful to the other party; that respect is manifested through observance of established conventions and good taste. Does it sound too difficult? Please do not panic, the Japanese are in many ways very much like us. You can solve most of the problems by using your good sense, perhaps as much as 80 percent of the time. There is always that remaining 20 percent, however, and this appendix is written to give pointers for just such occasions.

Dress Code

If in doubt, be on the formal side. Casual attire may be fine at your country club or at home, but not for serious business transactions or socializing in Japan. For men this means a two-piece suit (yes, two-piece; somehow, three-piece suits are not in vogue in Japan) of conservative color, usually dark blue or gray and often striped. For women, conservative business suits worn in the States are generally acceptable, but color selection is wider than for men. Always remember this: as a foreigner (*gaijin*) you stand out quite a bit. If you choose to wear something off color you call too much attention to yourself, and that can be considered a sign of disrespect. So, in color selection, play it safe. For men, polyester must never be worn. Wool or wool blend even in the summer is a must for business suits. Women cannot always avoid polyester, and you may prefer a good silk dress or a dress of natural blend that is not body clinging. Exercise your good taste in this instance.

Shirts are uniformly white, but this rule does not apply to women's blouses. The Japanese word for men's business shirts is *waishatsu*, which came from the English words "white shirts." Be sure to have a subdued tie to go along with your conservative suit and white shirt.

For men, shoes are almost uniformly black. They must be impeccably shined. Unlike in European countries, loafers are acceptable because you are expected to remove your shoes many times a day in Japanese surroundings. This raises another issue some gaijin may overlook. Always wear a good pair of matching socks or non-running hose. You do not want to go to someone's home or a Japanese restaurant and be embarrassed when you must remove your shoes.

Meeting a Japanese Friend for the First Time

Have you secured a proper introduction before coming to Japan? The importance of having a proper introduction cannot be overemphasized. One day I was in the headquarters of the Keidanren (Federation of Economic Associations). As I was chatting with one of its directors, he casually mentioned that many American governors had sat on the chair on which I was sitting. Then he wore a puzzled expression and said, "Some of your American governors just walked in here and demanded to see Mr. Inayama (who was then its president). Oh, they did not get to see him. How could they do it without an appropriate introduction!"

(If your company is deeply involved in Japanese affairs, securing an appropriate introduction should pose no problem. If it is not, consult your bank, which may be able to get you in touch with its correspondent bank in Japan, who in turn can provide some needed assistance. Or if your state already has a representative office in Tokyo, you can probably use their services.)

Meishi

One of the most important pieces of paper you need in Japan is your business calling card (in Japanese, *meishi*). It must contain your name, affiliation, title, company's address and telephone. You may include your home address and phone number if you so desire. This information must be printed in English on one side and in Japanese transliteration on the other. You may include your company's logo, but please do not make it too conspicuous. The Japanese always prefer understatement.

Here are some rules to keep in mind when exchanging your *meishi* with someone you meet for the first time:[1]

1. Try to present your own *meishi* before the other party starts the process — this is to show your respect toward the other party.

2. Hold your *meishi* with both hands, but if you must use only one hand, use your right hand.

3. Look at the other party (but not staring in his eyes) and bow about 30 degrees when you present your *meishi*. Make sure that the right side is up for him so he can read it as he receives it.

4. When you receive the other party's *meishi*, use both hands and bow.

Introducing and Being Introduced

You introduce the person who is lower in rank to the one who is higher in rank first. In Japan there is a custom of never using honorifics for persons from your own company when referring to them to persons from another company. Thus a Japanese salesman may introduce his president, "This is Imai, our president."

When you are called upon to introduce superiors from your own company, keep in mind this Japanese custom. More likely than not, you will be using English, so say simply "This is Roger Thomas, our group executive for Far East operations, and this is David Armstrong, our chairman of the board." Never say "This is Doctor David Armstrong." As you introduce your superiors, turn the palm of your hand up to indicate which person you are referring to. (No fingering please!) Let your superiors exchange their *meishi* first.

Some Americans have adopted the Japanese custom of affixing -san to another person's name. Smith-san means Mr. Smith. Do not make the mistake of affixing -san when you are introducing or referring to anyone from your own company.

When you are introduced to a large group, such as at a banquet, you stand up and bow about 30 degrees. Do not wave your hand(s) as politicians do in this country.

The Art of Bowing

When Japanese company employees see one another in the corridor or hallway, they usually greet each other with a light bow of about 15 degrees. This is not the bow you use when you meet your Japanese counterpart. For most occasions, a normal bow of about 30 degrees will suffice. However, if someone has done you a big favor and you want to say thank you from the bottom of your heart, you must treat him with a deep bow of 45 degrees. You do the same when apologizing for something.

How do you know you are bowing about 30 or 45 degrees? For

a 30-degree bow, gaze at a point about two yards from your feet, and for a 45-degree bow, look at a point about one yard from your feet. When your eyes have reached that point, you have completed your bow.

Remember when you bow to keep the back of your shoes together with the tips about five inches apart. Also your motion must be slow and deliberate. A quick motion to reach the 30-degree angle and a quick return to the full standing posture make you look like a toy soldier.

Have you ever seen some Japanese bowing while speaking on the phone? They are taught to do just that, and that act of bowing to the person unseen somehow induces the use of more polite language while speaking. It is not a bad custom.

You may prefer a handshake as a red-blooded American, but to bow or not to bow should not be a question in Japan. Yes, you may shake hands if an occasion calls for it, but please remember the following:

1. Ambassador Mike Mansfield is a great practitioner of bowing, and the Japanese public loves it. That single act of behaving like a Japanese has endeared him to them.

2. Here is what one CEO says: "Oh yes, I am happy to shake hands with my American friends, but when American businessmen visit me and adopt our custom of bowing, I know that they have studied our customs and culture. It makes me feel kinder toward them." Need I say more?

Meeting Your Japanese Friend in His Office

Here are some do's and don'ts:

1. Button the first button on your suit.

2. Do not cross your arms or legs.

3. Americans have a reputation for being loud. Don't give

your host any reason to confirm that view through your visit.

4. Do not start smoking before your host does. Don't light up or even try to offer your own cigarette unless your host clearly indicates that he intends to smoke.

5. If your first visit includes an exchange of gifts (*omiyage*), do not open the gift given to you in front of your host. You bow and thank him and keep your curiosity subdued. Nor should you insist that he open your gift.

Now assuming that a Japanese businessman is visiting your office, either in Japan or in the United States, let the above rules also guide you. Care must be taken especially on the matter of crossing your arms or legs. That posture will make you appear condescending or not serious enough about the matter you are discussing. If you have adopted the Japanese custom of giving a gift, try to have it gift wrapped.

Many American executives love to sit on their favorite large chairs to discuss their business dealing *ex cathedra*. Do not do it when your Japanese visitors are around. If possible, rearrange your office in such a way that your guests will occupy the seats of honor, those furthest from the door.

Meeting and Sending Off Guests

When you visit a Japanese businessman, he will usually walk to the elevator on his floor to send you off. Just before the door closes he bows to you. Don't forget to return the bow. You cannot substitute for it by waving your hand.

Often your host or his representatives will send you off at their gate, and they will remain there until your car is out of sight. If you are not the driver, chances are you will be sitting in the back seat. Before the car starts, open your window and bow to the host to thank him again. Do not close your window until the sending-off party is out of sight (unless it is raining hard).

From time to time, your host may ask his chauffeur to take you to your hotel or another destination. Have a thousand yen or two ready for the chauffeur, and give it to him when you disembark. (You can say that it is for his coffee break or cigarettes.) He will say "No" the first time, but you must insist, and he will take it. Remember, he must return to his post right away in that nasty Japanese traffic.

Place of Honor

In a car, the first one in and the last one out occupies the place of honor. If the car is driven by a chauffeur or a taxi driver, the seat immediately behind the driver is the place of honor. This means that you will be sitting on the right-hand side of the car. (In Japan, the steering wheel is on the right-hand side of the car. As in England, they drive on the left side of the road.) In a privately owned car, if the owner drives, the place of honor is next to him in the front seat.

If your host accompanies you in his chauffeur-driven car, he will ask you to enter the car first (usually from the left-hand side and it takes a little maneuvering). You can decline it politely, but if he insists, you can take the honored seat the second time. This is so because you are his guest. If your host outranks you in age and position by a substantial margin, however, you can insist that he take the seat of honor.

At the Banquet, Japanese Style

The seat of honor in a Japanese banquet room (*ozashiki*) is the seat furthest from the entryway and closest to the alcove (*tokonoma*) graced with a scroll and/or flower arrangement (*ikebana*). When there are many guests, the guest of honor is seated in the center of a row of seats closest to the alcove. The second most desirable seat is immediately next to him to the right (or to his left if facing him), and the third one is next to him to the left.

If you are invited to a Japanese banquet, your host has probably worked out carefully the seating arrangement ahead of time, so you can accept the arrangement that will place you in the seat of honor. Politely decline it at least once, however, to show your humility. In the event there is an elder present who is respected by all, it may be good for you to yield the place of honor to him. Do not overdo your act of declining, however. You do not want to engage in a contest of who is the humblest of all. An important consideration is how you, your host and other guests enjoy the evening together.

When sitting in a Japanese banquet room, remember the following.

1. You will be provided a *zabuton* (floor cushion) on which to sit. The first position you assume is that of *seiza*, which requires that your hips touch the soles of your feet. You take that position first, but your host is generous to foreigners. You will be asked to relax, and thereafter you can sit cross-legged. This position applies to men only, however. For women, the relaxed position is to have both soles of the feet to either side of the hips. When you sit cross-legged or with soles of the feet to one side of the hips, you can position your legs alternately to make it more comfortable.

2. Prior to the start of a traditional Japanese banquet, if someone comes to greet you formally, you should leave the *zabuton*, assume the *seiza* position on the *tatami* floor and bow. (This position would bring your forehead close to the floor with each of your palms placed to each side of your head. Practice this a few times before you accept an invitation to a Japanese banquet.) You cannot remain on the *zabuton* to bow. To do so is just like remaining seated on your chair to greet an important person whose favor is essential to your success. You do not take such matters casually in the United States nor should you do so

in Japan. This practice applies equally to men and women.

3. Your host may ask if you prefer *sake* (rice wine), wine, beer or hard liquor. You may show your preference, but it is best to leave the choice to your host to get an evening of genuine Japanese experience. (If you prefer soft drink, do not hesitate to ask for it.) Don't drink excessively. It is true that in Japan, public drunkenness is tolerated. The social convention allows colleagues to get drunk and, while drunk, criticize their superiors and other colleagues. This has served the function of a safety valve in a highly structured, rigid hierarchical society. The same does not apply to guests, however. When colleagues get drunk and misbehave, it can be tolerated because they are all members of "one big family." Anything done within the family (*uchi*) is fine. When you are an outsider (*soto*), however, misbehavior or even mild drunkenness is never viewed with favor.

4. When rice is served in a bowl, never stick your chopsticks straight in the rice in the upright position. It creates an eerie reminder of food offerings to the dead, with several incense sticks burning. "Let us eat, drink and be merry, for tomorrow we die," you may want to say, but I doubt your host would appreciate a reminder of man's mortality at his banquet table.

Some American anthropologists rhapsodize about Japanese tolerance for drunkenness and, according to them, the first order of business for a foreign businessman is to learn how to get drunk like the Japanese. If true, these anthropologists must be traveling in circles different from mine. Many of the CEOs and company directors I have known consume alcoholic beverages only moderately. There is a gentleman in his eighties who has served as CEO for a major broadcasting company for many years. When hosting a meeting for me, I noticed that he did not touch his wine glass. I asked if he did drink, and his answer was to the point: "I never touch that stuff. I allow my employees to get drunk, though, and I never promoted anyone who spoke against the company while drunk." Here goes the myth of Japan's toleration!

Geisha

Assuming that your Japanese contact has found out that you are accompanied by your wife and has invited you and your wife to a geisha party, should both of you go? The answer is: you must go without your wife.

A word to American wives: you should be aware that there is nothing wrong with an invitation to a geisha party. The main purpose of having the geisha is to pick up slack in conversation. These geisha entertain their guests with conversation while serving food and drink. That is about all you can expect from a geisha party and it can get rather boring. Japanese businessmen want your husbands to be there because they are process-oriented, and they want a chance to know your husbands better before they start business dealings. You are not sending your husbands off to a den of iniquity.

Now that question is settled, why must the wife decline the invitation? The simple fact is that in Japan wives almost never accompany their husbands to social or business functions. Your Japanese contact has made a concession to the American custom by inviting both of you, but frankly he would prefer that your wife not come. He may still insist that your wife accept the invitation just to be polite, but your solution can be deceptively simple. Buy your wife a ticket to a performance of the Grand Kabuki, or to the visiting Kirov ballet for that evening, and then tell your Japanese contact how sorry your wife is in not being able to accept his kind invitation. He will accept your excuse graciously, with a secret sigh of relief!

When Visiting a Private Home

Just as in the United States, it is a good practice to make an appointment before you pay a visit to a private home. Here are some do's and don'ts in Japan.

1. If you wear an overcoat, remove it before you enter the

front door. Otherwise your host or hostess may come to help you remove your overcoat as you enter. Your action obviates that.

2. When you visit a private home, you usually take something to the family. This is called *omiyage*. This word originally meant a special product from the home area of the visitor, but today it simply means a gift. If you have something nice from the States, so much the better. If not, buy something such as a box of cake (Japanese or Western) or basket of fruit in the neighborhood where you are staying. When you enter the door, give your *omiyage* to the hostess.

In Japan, packaged pieces are often assembled in odd numbers. You may, for example, receive a set of five cups (not six). Odd numbers are supposed to represent *yang*, or the positive force in the world and bring good luck. Speaking of luck, never give your friend a gift assembled in a set of four. The word for the number "four" in Japanese is *shii*, which sounds like the word meaning "death."

3. Most Japanese homes have an entryway where shoes are still worn, but shoes must be removed before entering other parts of the home. You face your host (or hostess) while removing your shoes. Do not kick off your shoes but use your hand(s) gently. After you step on the raised part of the floor, take a kneeling position to replace your shoes to the corner of the entryway after turning them with tips facing the front door.

4. When you step on the raised wooden floor, you will be provided with a pair of house slippers. These are to be worn on the wooden floor only (including the Western-style living room), but not on the *tatami*-matted rooms. You must remove them before you enter any of the *tatami* rooms. If you should use their bathroom, be sure to remove your house slippers and use the slippers provided for the bathroom. Do not forget to change back to the house slippers when you leave the bathroom.

5. When you are led to the living room by someone other than your host, you will be asked to take your seat. It is impolite, however, to sit in a seat of honor to greet your host when

he enters. To avoid this, you may want to remain standing and look at the art objects or flower arrangements. If you choose to sit, stand up when the host enters.

6. In a Japanese room, it is more polite to sit while waiting. Standing there looks rather awkward. Remember to get off the *zabuton* and bow to the host from the *seiza* position on the *tatami* floor when he enters.

7. Japanese tea is served in cups without a handle. You use the fingers of your right hand to hold the cup, while letting the fingers of your left hand support the bottom of the cup. Some men may prefer an informal style of using only the right hand. You can observe how your host does it, and follow his lead. For women, though, good deportment calls for the use of both hands.

8. When invited to a Japanese home, it is considered impolite to look at the kitchen. On a rare occasion, American women may be invited to a private home for a meal. They can offer to help with the dishes, but must not insist on doing it. If met by a polite "No," let the matter rest there. This prohibition does not apply if you are living with the family.

9. When you leave a Japanese home, do not sit on the raised floor to put your shoes on. Step down on the earthen or tiled floor, which constitutes the home's entryway, face your host (and hostess) as you put your shoes on. They will usually hand you a long shoe horn. You can use it and, when you are through, hand it to another guest (if there is one), or replace it in the corner of the entryway. If you cannot find an appropriate place to put it, give it back to the hostess with a slight bow. An important thing to remember is not to show your back to your host and hostess. You bow once more (30 degrees) to thank them before you depart.

An abbreviated version of the above process is to step in your shoes, turn around before you complete the process with or without the help of the shoe horn, and then bow to thank your host. If you are not comfortable with the first example, try at least this much.

Making a Presentation in Japan

A rule of thumb is again to use common sense. What goes well in the United States usually goes well in Japan, but please note the following:

1. Before you start your presentation, and just before you step on the podium, bow to the audience (30 degrees). When you finish your presentation, step off the podium and bow. If you have presentation materials, lay them aside and free your hands before you bow.

2. Keep your jacket on and never put your hands in your pocket.

3. Do not smoke as you talk.

4. Make your presentation lively and watch closely the audience reaction. However, this does not mean that you can make your presentation too informal. You may have seen the movie "Gung Ho." In it is told the story of a representative from a small U.S. town who successfully woos a major automaker from Japan to start operating a failing plant in his hometown. That remains in the realm of fiction. The air of informality the representative conveys in the movie would not allow him to reach first base in real life.

If It Is Your Turn to Host

If you have a sizeable number of people you want to invite, should you have a cocktail party? My advice is "No." There are several good reasons for this advice:

1. Imagine yourself being a Japanese for a moment. You are shorter in stature than those Americans you meet. You naturally feel uncomfortable when you must meet a large number of them, especially if nobody sits down.

2. As a Japanese you have always been taught that you are not supposed to put your hand in your pocket. Now imagine

having a cocktail glass in one hand — where should the other hand be? With your left hand hanging stiffly and not gainfully employed, you will have a difficult time concentrating on small talk and business overtures.

3. The physical discomfort that your Japanese friends feel may look insignificant to you, but please remember a successful business talk can begin only if you can make your counterparts feel at ease. A cocktail party does not seem to accomplish this task.

Thus if you must have a large number of guests, consider having a smorgasbord party (which the Japanese call Vikings), and make sure that there are chairs for your guests and associates to sit and talk. Even when you do not want to have a heavy meal, it is still better to place emphasis on food rather than on drinks.

Better still, utilize the Japanese principle of "less is more." Why not consider holding a small dinner party to allow you and a few of your important Japanese contacts to get to know one another?

The next question is where to hold such a dinner party. If you know Japan well, I mean really well, then there is nothing to prevent you from inviting your guests to a good Japanese restaurant where the meals are served on the *ozashiki* with the *tatami*-matted floor. If you are a novice in this area, however, do not try it. Some of the most reputable restaurants require a proper introduction before you can secure the right *ozashiki*, and the cost is steeper than in other restaurants. If you try to go to a good Japanese restaurant, you are liable to make many mistakes.

Your best choice may well be some good French restaurants, which get star billings. Some good Chinese restaurants can also be effective. (For both, but especially for the latter, be sure to request a private dining room.)

If you are planning to invite a number of guests from different Japanese companies, be sure to make an appropriate seating arrangement ahead of time.

If your guests are from the same company, they probably know instinctively who must occupy the honored seat and the problem may not arise. In the case of guests from different companies, consider the importance to you of the respective companies and the positions the guests hold in these companies as well as the ages of these individuals to determine the seating arrangement. A handy introduction to Japanese companies is available in English, entitled *Japan Company Handbook*, published semiannually by Toyo Keizai. The book contains the names of companies whose stocks are traded in Japan's various stock exchanges, as well as names of their company directors. Information concerning individuals can be found in *Nippon Shinshiroku*, Japan's counterpart of our *Who's Who in America*. Unfortunately the text is in Japanese but, for a very important meeting, it may be worth asking someone to check these entries for you.

In a Chinese restaurant, a banquet is normally served on a round table, and mistakes in seating arrangements are less noticeable. Still, the general rule of thumb is that the seat furthest from the door is the place of honor, and you can start from there. In a Japanese restaurant, follow the seating arrangement given in *At the Banquet, Japanese Style* above. In a French restaurant, be guided by the procedures you normally follow at home in the United States.

Finally, if you want to give a gift to each of the guests, wait until the time of their departure. You may want to provide transportation for some of your guests for their return home. You must arrange to have the fare prepaid. Some taxi and chauffeured limousine (called *haiya* — cars hired) companies accept chits issued by you on the form they provide, and you can give these chits to your guests in lieu of prepayment. If you are alone, the best place to obtain information concerning these chits is the front desk of your hotel. If you have a Japanese associate, ask him to make these necessary arrangements.

Language

In business dealings, even if you know some Japanese, it is

best that you conduct your negotiations in English. It avoids later misunderstanding. It is also good to have a translator or translators present. It allows you time to rethink some of the major issues. However, on purely social occasions, try to use some Japanese words. Listed below are some most obvious ones:[2]

Ohayoo gozaimasu means "good morning." Memorize and use the entire phrase. To shorten it to *ohayoo* is rather impolite.

Kon-nichiwa means "good afternoon." This is the full phrase.

Konbanwa means "good evening." This is again the full phrase.

Arigato gozaimashita is "thank you," which incidentally is its past tense. You use this form immediately after someone has done something nice for you. Its present tense is *arigato gozaimasu*, often used in anticipation rather than after the fact.

Doomo is a very convenient catch-all phrase. It can mean "thank you," when a gift is given to you or when someone has done a favor for you. When you step on someone's toe and want to say "I am sorry," the word can be *doomo*. This word's versatility was demonstrated by Richard Chamberlain when he played the role of Anjin-san in the NBC mini-series *Shogun*. By repeating *doomo* frequently, he gave an appearance of being fluent in Japanese.

When you meet someone for the first time, you say "*Hajimemashite*," meaning "I am happy to make your acquaintance." This phrase can be used when you give the other party your *meishi* (business calling card). You can follow that with another phrase, "*Yoroshiku onegai itashimasu*." This last phrase defies translation. We simply do not have words comparable to it. Consider it a nice phrase to be used when starting a new business association or reaffirming existing ties. Thus this phrase can be used when the other party gives you his *meishi*.

At a banquet or even just meeting for lunch, before you start, bow lightly to your host and say "*Itadakimasu*." It means you appreciate the opportunity of partaking of the food provided by him. After the meal, bow lightly again and say "*Gochisoosama deshita.*" It means "Thank you for the delicious meal." If you are the host, you can ask your guests to start by saying, *"Doozo"* (please) with a bow. When the meal is completed, say *"Osomatsusama deshita"* (Sorry, this is rather inelegant fare), again with a bow.

There are times you may have to use the bathroom. The phrase to use is *"Otearai wa doko desuka?"* (Where is the toilet, please?) or *"Otearai o tsukawasete itadakemasenka?"* (May I use your bathroom?). You address these questions to the person who is lower in rank, and not to your host directly.

At Ease, Please!

Reviewing what I have written, I find that I have not always acted according to the rules of etiquette given here. The Japanese people are rather forgiving when it comes to mistakes made by foreigners. It is your goodwill that counts and not your superficial observance of these rules. So please relax and have a good and successful trip to Japan.

Sayoonara!

Notes

Chapter 1

1. Kunitomo Ryuichi, *Kansai-gata kigyo no mirai senryaku* (Future strategies of the Kansai-type industries) (Tokyo: Paru Shuppan, 1984), 22.

2. Ibid., 23-24.

3. Takara Belmont, *Sekai wa hitotsu: Yoshikawa Hidenobu to Takara Gurupu* (The world is one: Yoshikawa Hidenobu and the Takara Group) (Osaka: 1984), supplemented by interviews with various company workers and executives, including Yoshikawa Takatoshi, the son of the founder.

4. Interview with former prime minister Sato Eisaku, July 1972. I also met with textile traders in the summer of 1978 on this very issue.

5. Matsushita Konosuke, *Ketsudan no keiei* (Decisive management) (Kyoto: PHP, 1979), 207-208.

6. Nemoto's management philosophy is contained in his *Total Quality Control for Management*, trans. David Lu (Englewood Cliffs, N.J.: Prentice-Hall, 1987).

7. Credit for creating the Walkman should go to Morita. In his own words: "I knew from my own experience at home that young people cannot seem to live without music.... I had seen people with big tape players and radios perched on their shoulders blaring out music. [When] my daughter Naoko came home from a trip she ran upstairs before even greeting her mother and first put a cassette in her stereo.... I ordered our engineers to take one of our reliable small cassette tape recorders we called Pressman, strip out the recording circuit and the speaker, and replace them with a stereo amplifier...." From Akio Morita with Edwin M. Reingold and Mitsuko Shimamura, *Made in Japan: Akio Morita and Sony* (New York: E. P. Dutton, 1986), 79.

Chapter 2

1. David Halberstam, *The Reckoning* (New York: Morrow, 1986), 236 ff.

2. *See* David J. Lu, *Sources of Japanese History* (New York: McGraw-Hill, 1974), 2:270-275.

3. Nagamori Shigenobu, *Kiseki no jinzai ikusei-ho* (Miraculous method of human resources development) (Kyoto: PHP, 1984), 87-110.

4. Akio Morita with Edwin M. Reingold and Mitsuko Shimamura, *Made in Japan: Akio Morita and Sony* (New York: E. P. Dutton, 1986), 131, 149

5. See its two-volume *Kaisha no jumyo* (Life expectancy of companies) (Tokyo: Nihon Keizai, 1984-85).

6. My meeting with Mr. Tamaru took place one late summer afternoon in 1983. As the sun was about to set in the west with a commanding view from his office, I thought of a poem from the Manyoshu that Mr. Tamaru loved. It is by Princess Nukata:
   Going through the fields of wild flowers,
   The field reserved for the party of His Majesty.
   Has not the field ranger seen it?
   The waving of the sleeves of my Prince!
   It is a love song that has an expectant air, but with a tinge of loneliness. To be a corporate president is a lonely business. Those select few who occupy that position are certainly entitled to choose their own successors.

7. Toyoda Eiji, *Ketsudan* (Making decisions decisively) (Tokyo: Nippon Keizai Shimbunsha, 1985), 240-244.

Chapter 3

1. *See* David Lu, *Sources of Japanese History* (New York: McGraw-Hill, 1974), 2:80-82.

2. "Dentsu's Management Philosophy and Public Service Activities," Dentsu Information Series, June 1982.

3. Yoshida Tadao, *Ori-ori ni* (Occasional thoughts) (Tokyo: Rinjin shuppan, 1979), 16. Appropriately, Yoshida's two-volume official biography is entitled *Zen no junkan* (Recycling of goodness) (Tokyo, 1974).

4. Narushima Tadaaki, *Seibu no subete* (Everything about Seibu) (Tokyo: Nihon Jitsugyo, 1983), 25-27.

5. David Lu, op. cit., 1:251.

6. Hayashi Tatsuhiko, *Jitsuroku: iue gakko* (Iue school: records of a management philosophy that shaped Kansai managers) (Tokyo: Diamond, 1985), 173-174.

7. Odakyu traces its history back to 1923 when the company was established to lay a rail line between Shinjuku and Odawara, the entrance to the hot spring resort area of Hakone. During World War II, the company had to merge with other suburban rail lines by the decree of the government, but it became independent again in 1948. In the expansive postwar era, the Hakone area prospered. Odakyu established a "mountain climbing line" from Odawara to Hakone Yumoto in August 1950, laying its claim to the further development of the area. Seibu, however, also moved into the area aggressively. It had a prior claim, in a sense, that the company was first founded in 1920 to develop Hakone, even though it later expended more energy in the Ikebukuro area within Tokyo and in Karuizawa, the fashionable summer residence town for the elite of Tokyo. In any event, Seibu's mountain climbing bus lines along with other bus routes directly challenged Odakyu's established routes. A bitter conflict ensued between the two companies and a compromise plan was not worked out until 1961.

8. I am grateful to Hasegawa Takashi for suggesting that I study Odakyu. When I approached him in 1983 to ask which of the fourteen major privately owned railways I should study, Hasegawa recommended Odakyu without hesitation. "It is a good company," he said, "and besides, it has never had a strike that stopped its trains." Hasegawa was then the Transport Minister. He was also Labor Minister in 1974-75, and was credited with resolving one of the worst nationwide wage disputes during the spring offensive, following the first oil crisis. His suggestion came not just for the study of the railway company itself but also for the distinguished nature of the company's labor relations.

9. The term "rationalization" (in Japanese, *gorika*) is frequently used in Japanese writings to indicate activities undertaken to upgrade technology, improve quality and reduce cost. Additionally, it may also mean reorganizing and integrating an industry while engaged in the above mentioned activities.

10. Lee Iacocca, *Iacocca: An Autobiography* (New York: Bantam, 1984), 236.

11. *Centre Daily Times*, 4 January 1987, Sports section, reported by Jim Carlson, *Times* Sports Editor.

Chapter 4

1. Japan Management Association, ed., *Kanban: Just-in-Time at Toyota*, trans. David Lu (Cambridge: Productivity Press, 1986), 66-67.

2. Ibid., 133.

3. Japan Management Association, *Mazda no genba kakushin* (Mazda's workplace reform) (Tokyo: JMA Press, 1984), 99-104.

4. Kondo Hiroshi, *Toyota Shoho, Matsushita Shoho* (Toyotaism and Matsushitaism) (Tokyo: Nihon Jitsugyo, 1977), 135-137.

5. Kaoru Ishikawa, *What Is Total Quality Control? The Japanese Way*, trans. David Lu (Englewood Cliffs, N.J.: Prentice-Hall, 1985), 158.

6. Kono Tsutomu, *Tetsu wa Horobinai* (Iron shall remain forever) (Tokyo: Nippon Kogyo, 1983), 227.

Chapter 5

1. Karatsu Hajime, *TQC, Nihon no Chie* (TQC, The Wisdom of Japan) (Tokyo: JUSE Press, 1981), 6-7.

2. Kaoru Ishikawa, *What Is Total Quality Control? The Japanese Way*, trans. David Lu (Englewood Cliffs: Prentice-Hall, 1985), 44.

3. Ibid., 44.

4. Ibid., 107-108.

5. Ibid., 139-140.

6. Ibid., 147.

7. Nikkei Business, *Kaisha no jumyo* (Life expectancy of companies) (Tokyo: Nihon Keizai, 1984), vol. 1. The entire volume is devoted to the discussion of the thesis that most companies have only 30 years of life expectancy.

8. Kondo Hiroshi, *Toyota Shoho Matsushita Shoho* (Toyotaism and Matsushitaism) (Tokyo: Nihon Jitsugyo, 1977), 90-96. An informative analysis of Matsushita's management techniques can be found in Richard T. Pascale and Anthony G. Athos, *The Art of Japanese Management* (New York: Warner Books, 1981).

9. Kunitomo Ryuichi, *Inamori kazuo goroku ni miru kyocera kagekinaru seiko no himitsu* (Secrets of Kyocera's remarkable growth through the sayings of Inamori Kazuo) (Tokyo: Koshobo, 1985), 124-125.

10. New Seven Tool Study Group, *Yasashii shin QC nanatsu dogu: TQC suishin no tame* (Simplified seven new QC tools: For promoting TQC) (Tokyo: JUSE Press, 1984), 88-89.

Chapter 6

1. *Chugoku Shimbun*, Hiroshima's regional daily, published a series of articles about Mazda (then Toyo Kogyo, K. K.) from June 1, 1978 through March 2, 1979. The description appearing in this chapter is

largely based on these articles along with some interviews.

2. Sumitomo has generously rewarded some of its executives who have effectively reorganized client companies. The latest example is Komatsu Yasushi, named President of the Sumitomo Bank in 1985. A few years back, he accepted the thankless job of reorganizing Ataka, the bankrupt trading company. He succeeded in having more than a thousand of its employees transferred to another trading company, Ito Chu. In the process, Sumitomo received accolades for its responsible management as the "main bank."

3. *Sanyo denki sanjunen no ayumi* (Sanyo's first three decades, a company history) (Moriguchi: Sanyo, 1980), 199-200.

4. As quoted in Nikkei Business, *Kaisha no jumyo* 2:65

Chapter 7

1. Gil Burck, "International Business Machines," *Fortune* (January 1940), 40.

2. Kameoka Taro, *IBM no jinji kanri* (IBM's personnel policy) (Tokyo: Santenshobo, 1958) gives a detailed account of IBM Japan's personnel practices.

3. Some of these topics are discussed in the appendix. Please note appendix footnote 1.

4. Arakawa Susumu wrote a series of forty articles about IBM Japan in the *Nippon Kogyo Shimbun* from April 2, 1975. These are compiled in *Shashi Sowa* (Episodes from company history), from which some of the stories are taken.

5. Zaibatsu refers to prewar industrial conglomerates that were ordered dissolved by the GHQ due to their contributions to Japan's war effort.

6. The Japanese government's approach was in sharp contrast to that of the United States. What it had done would have been in contravention of the Sherman antitrust law. Meanwhile in America, both IBM and AT&T were subjects of almost endless antitrust suits by the Justice Department.

Chapter 8

1. *New York Times*, 11 Jan. 1987, Sunday Business section.

2. *New York Times*, 15 Jan. 1984, Sunday Business section.

3. *New York Times*, 11 Jan. 1987.

4. As quoted in David Halberstam, *The Reckoning* (New York: Morrow, 1986), 55.

5. Kunimoto Ryuichi, *Kyocera: kagekinaru seiko no himitsu* (Kyocera: secrets of its remarkable success) (Tokyo: Kou Shobo, 1985), 156-160.

6. Ira C. Magaziner and Robert B. Reich, *Minding America's Business: The Decline and Rise of the American Economy* (New York: Random House, 1982), 255, 329-363.

7. Ezra Vogel, *Comeback: Case by Case: Building the Resurgence of American Business* (New York: Simon and Schuster, 1985), 280 ff.

8. "Bounties are sometimes not only the best, but the only proper expedient, for uniting the encouragement of a new object of agriculture, with that of a new object of manufacture.... The true way to conciliate these two interests, is to lay a duty on foreign *manufactures* of the material, the growth of which is desired to be encouraged, and to apply the produce of that duty by way of bounty, either upon the production of the material itself or upon its manufacture at home or upon both. In this disposition of the thing, the Manufacturer commences his enterprise under every advantage...; he has a motive of interest to prefer the domestic Commodity, if of equal quality, even at a higher price than the foreign, so long as the difference of price is any thing short of the bounty which is allowed upon the article....

"The continuance of bounties on manufactures long established must almost always be of questionable policy: Because a presumption would arise in every such Case, that there were natural and inherent impediments to success. But in new undertakings, they are as justifiable, as they are oftentimes necessary....There is not purpose, to which public money can be more beneficially applied, than to the acquisition of a new and useful branch of industry; no Consideration more valuable than a permanent addition to the general stock of productive labour." From "Report on Manufactures, Hamilton's Final Version" in Harold C. Syrett, editor, *The Papers of Alexander Hamilton*, vol. X, December 1971-January 1972, New York, Columbia University Press, 1966, pp. 300-301.

9. These are summary statements from Kiuchi Nobutane, *Kuni no kosei* (Individuality of a nation) (Tokyo: Diamond Sha, 1985), published in December of that year to commemorate his eighty-eighth birthday.

10. Inayama Toshiro, speech delivered to the Contemporary Affairs Council, Naigai News Co., September 16, 1985, recorded in *Sekai to nippon* booklet No. 472.

Appendix

1. In this and in other examples cited in this appendix, I have been greatly aided by the fine *Manual for Marketing Personnel* issued by IBM Japan. Entitled *Eigyobuin no Reigi to Kikubari*, it shows IBM Japan's commitment to making the company into a genuinely "Japanese company,"

where Japanese practices are carefully observed.

2. If you would like to study the language in earnest, try *Business Japanese*, prepared by Nissan Motor Company. It is distributed by Bonjin Co., Ltd., 6F Kojimachi 6 Chome Bldg., 6-2, Kojimachi, Chiyoda-ku, Tokyo 102, Japan.

About the Author

David J. Lu was born in Taiwan in 1928. He learned Japanese as a child during the occupation of the island in World War II and received a Japanese education through high school. After graduating in economics from National Taiwan University, he received his Masters and Ph.D. degrees from Columbia University in international law and relations. Now an American citizen, he is currently Professor of History and Japanese Studies and Director of the Center for Japanese Studies at Bucknell University.

Dr. Lu writes regularly for the weekly *Sekai to Nippon* (World and Japan) on U.S. and international affairs. He has lectured extensively in Japan and the United States, where he has served as a consultant for the Foreign Service Institute of the Department of State, the U.S. Department of Education, and various state departments in Pennsylvania.

He has maintained close contact with Japan's political and economic leaders, including two prime ministers — the late Sato Eisaku, Nobel Prize winner, and Fukuda Takeo, widely credited with Japan's economic recovery. He ran unsuccessfully for U.S. Congress from Pennsylvania's 17th district in 1976 and 1980.

His books published in the United States include: *Sources of Japanese History*, 2 vol. (New York: McGraw-Hill, 1974); *From the Marco Polo Bridge to Pearl Harbor* (Public Affairs Press,

1961) — published in Japan by Hara Shobo in 1967; and (as editor and contributor) *Perspectives on Japan's External Relations: Views from America* (Bucknell University, 1982).

Published translations include: Japan Management Association, ed., *Kanban and Just-In-Time at Toyota* (Cambridge, MA: Productivity Press, 1986); Kaoru Ishikawa, *What Is Total Quality Control? The Japanese Way* (Englewood Cliffs, NJ: Prentice-Hall, 1985); Katsumi Usui and Yukuhiko Hata, *The China Quagmire: Japan's Expansion on the Asian Continent, 1933-1941* (New York: Columbia University Press, 1983); and Masao Nemeto, *Total Quality Control for Management* (Englewood Cliffs, NJ: Prentice-Hall, 1987).

Books published in Japan include: *The Great Society that the Pioneers Built: A Bicentennial History of the United States* (Tokyo: Zenponnsha, 1976); and *The Life and Times of Foreign Minister Matsuoka Yosuke, 1880-1946* (Tokyo: TBS Britannica, 1981).

Index

COMPANIES

KANTO-TYPE

● TOKYO

Dentsu
Fujitsu
Hitachi
Honda Motors
Kabushiki Shimbun
Komatsu
Mitsubishi
Naigai News
NEC
Nippon Telephone and
 Telegraph (NTT)
Odakyu (Railway)
Pentel
Seibu
Sony

● KAWASAKI

Nippon Kokan

● YOKOHAMA

Nissan Motors

INDEPENDENT

● KUROBE

YKK

● MISAWA

Komaki Hot Spring Spa

AMERICAN

IBM Japan, in Tokyo, with
 plants in Fujisawa
 and Yasu
Coca Cola, Tokyo

M A P

O F

J A P A N

Kurobe

Yokohama

Hofu   Hiroshima   Kobe   Kyoto   Yasu   Haruhi   Fujisawa
                                                Nagoya
                          Iyo Mishima   Toyoda City
                    Osaka   Toyohashi
         KYUSHU   SHIKOKU

Moriguchi   Kadoma

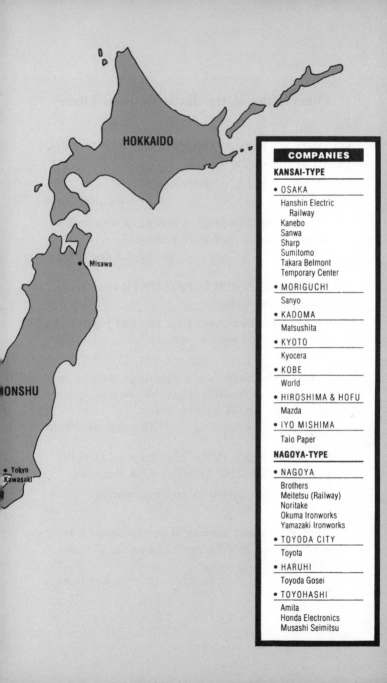

HOKKAIDO

Misawa

MONSHU

Tokyo
Kawasaki

COMPANIES

KANSAI-TYPE

- OSAKA

  Hanshin Electric
      Railway
  Kanebo
  Sanwa
  Sharp
  Sumitomo
  Takara Belmont
  Temporary Center

- MORIGUCHI

  Sanyo

- KADOMA

  Matsushita

- KYOTO

  Kyocera

- KOBE

  World

- HIROSHIMA & HOFU

  Mazda

- IYO MISHIMA

  Taio Paper

NAGOYA-TYPE

- NAGOYA

  Brothers
  Meitetsu (Railway)
  Noritake
  Okuma Ironworks
  Yamazaki Ironworks

- TOYODA CITY

  Toyota

- HARUHI

  Toyoda Gosei

- TOYOHASHI

  Amita
  Honda Electronics
  Musashi Seimitsu

Other Titles in the Tuttle Business Library

SECOND TO NONE: AMERICAN COMPANIES IN
JAPAN *by Robert C. Christopher*

> "A timely, highly readable book."
> —*New York Times*

> "Rare is the European or American who under-
> stands Japan as well as this author."
> —*Nihon Keizei Shimbun*

JAPAN: THE FRAGILE SUPERPOWER (2nd revised
edition) *by Frank Gibney*

> "One of the best panoramic views of Japan to have
> been published within memory."
> —*The New Republic*

> "One of the finest books written on Asia by any
> American . . . readable, enjoyable, exciting, powerful,
> important, a book written to last."
> —Theodore H. White

TRADING PLACES: HOW AMERICA ALLOWED
JAPAN TO TAKE THE LEAD *by Clyde Prestowitz*

> "Full of fresh anecdotes and information."
> —*Time*

> "For any serious student of our economic relations
> with Japan, Clyde Prestowitz's book is a 'must
> read'!"
> —Lee Iacocca

SETTING UP & OPERATING A BUSINESS IN JAPAN: A HANDBOOK FOR THE FOREIGN BUSINESSMAN *by Helene Thian*

"A unique handbook, speaking to the key issues and drawing on the experiences of veterans at the Japan business game."

—James C. Abegglen

MITI AND THE JAPANESE MIRACLE: THE GROWTH OF INDUSTRIAL POLICY, 1925–1975 *by Chalmers Johnson*

"Johnson sets out to explain and in the process to demystify the reasons for Japanese economic success by concentrating on the one institution which perhaps more than any other has been responsible for achieving that success: the Ministry of International Trade and Industry (MITI). It is a daunting task admirably undertaken by Johnson . . . who has produced a rich, suggestive, and stimulating book."

—*Far Eastern Economic Review*

THE JAPANESE MIND: THE GOLIATH EXPLAINED *by Robert C. Christopher*

"A very perceptive, well-informed, interesting and also amusing look at contemporary Japan and its position in the world."

—Edwin O. Reischauer

"Christopher's significant book drives home a centrally important message: not technique but culture is the key to Japan's success."

—Zbigniew Brzezinski

HOW TO DO BUSINESS WITH THE JAPANESE: A STRATEGY FOR SUCCESS *by Mark Zimmerman*

"Precisely what an able Western businessman coming to Japan wants to know, by an astute, hard-working business leader who got the nuances right."

—Ezra F. Vogel

THE JAPANESE COMPANY *by Rodney Clark*

"Mr. Clark has written an excellent analysis [of the Japanese company] that should stand the tests of time and competition to become a definitive work in the genre."

—*Wall Street Journal*

KAISHA: THE JAPANESE CORPORATION *by James C. Abegglen and George Stalk, Jr.*

"If I were a U.S. manager trying to understand the anatomy of a Japanese racer breathing hard at my shoulder, I'd read this book."

—*Wall Street Journal*